HISTORY NOTES

James L. Halverson

Judson College

A STUDY GUIDE TO ACCOMPANY

THE HERITAGE OF WORLD CIVILIZATIONS

VOLUME ONE: TO 1650

TEACHING AND LEARNING CLASSROOM EDITION
BRIEF SECOND EDITION

Albert M. Craig

William A. Graham

Donald Kagan

Steven Ozment

Frank M. Turner

PEARSON

Prentice
Hall

Upper Saddle River, New Jersey 07458

© 2005 by PEARSON EDUCATION, INC.
Upper Saddle River, New Jersey 07458

10 9 8 7 6 5 4 3 2

ISBN 0-13-191575-4

Printed in the United States of America

TABLE OF CONTENTS

Chapter One
The Birth of Civilization

Practice Test

1. Culture is best defined as
    a. the way in which many people live in urban centers, have mastered the art of smelting metals, and have developed a method of writing
    b. the ways of living built up by a group and passed on from one generation to another
    c. a society in which the population engages in abstract thought and promotes policies of peace rather than war
    d. the complex interrelationships among human beings which result in writing, literature, and cities

2. Civilization is a form of human culture marked by
    a. division of labor, animal husbandry, and writing
    b. urbanism, hunting, and gathering
    c. settled agriculture, stone tools, and music
    d. urbanism, metallurgy, and writing

3. Which of the following was <u>not</u> an early center of civilization?
    a. Rhine River
    b. Nile River
    c. Yellow River
    d. Mesopotamia

4. The Code of Hammurabi was
    a. an outline of religious practice
    b. a body of civil and criminal law
    c. the moral teaching of Hammurabi
    d. a system of writing developed by the Babylonians

5. The uniformity of building construction and city layout in Harappan excavation sites suggests
    a. an integrated economic system and good internal communications
    b. a lack of imagination and creativity in the culture
    c. the geographical isolation of the region
    d. both a and b

6. In Egypt, the king
    a. was appointed by the nobility
    b. enforced written law codes
    c. was considered a god
    d. ruled through priests

7. Mesopotamian religion focused on
    a. discovering the will and intentions of the gods
    b. preparing for the afterlife
    c. faith and the rejection of omens
    d. the reading of oracle bones

8. Religion
    a. presented an optimistic view of the afterworld
    b. played a large part in the literature and art of Mesopotamia
    c. emphasized human sacrifice as an integral part of religious celebration
    d. both a and c

9. Sumerian and Babylonian government was
    a. centralized
    b. decentralized
    c. combined political and religious authority
    d. both a and c

10. Sargon
    a. established a dynasty that ruled Sumer and Akkad for two centuries
    b. found ways of controlling the Tigris and Euphrates rivers
    c. conquered the "cedar forests of Lebanon"
    d. both a and c

11. Cuneiform
    a. was a writing system invented by the Sumerians
    b. developed into hieroglyphics
    c. was written on papyrus
    d. both b and c

12. The Egyptian period of greatest pharaonic authority was the
    a. Old Kingdom   c. New Kingdom
    b. Middle Kingdom   d. First Intermediate Period

13. The New Kingdom was began when
    a. the pyramids were built
    b. the Kyksos were driven out
    c. Egypt conquered the Hittites
    d. both a and b

14. *Veda*
    a. means "text" and was the sacred book of the Aryans
    b. is a language that belongs to the Indo-European group
    c. is a collective term for Indian holy texts
    d. none of the above

15. The characteristic political institution of Bronze Age China was
    a. the agricultural state   c. a republic
    b. the city-state   d. a democracy

16. The supreme "Deity Above" belonged to the
    a. Toltecs   c. Eastern Chou dynasty
    b. Vedic Aryans   d. Shang Chinese

17. Which of the following contributed to the rise of large territorial states in China?
    a. expansion of population and agricultural lands
    b. rise of commerce
    c. changes in military tactics and organization
    d. all of the above

18. One of the most important developments in the rise of civilizations in the Americas was
    a. the domestication of cattle
    b. the cultivation of maize
    c. conquest of indigenous peoples
    d. both a and c

19. The first strong, long-lasting state to arise in the Americas arose in
     a. the Andean region
     b. Mesoamerica
     c. the North American Southwest
     d. both a and c

20. The Hittites created a strong, centralized kingdom in
     a. Mesopotamia
     b. the Indus valley
     c. Turkey
     d. Mesoamerica

21. Which of the following methods was used by the Assyrians to systematically exploit conquered territory?
     a. scattering populations away from their homelands
     b. stationing garrisons in conquered territory
     c. ruling through local governments
     d. both a and b

22. The central focus of Vedic religion was
     a. monotheism
     b. ritual sacrifice
     c. water purification
     d. the flooding of the Nile

23. The Mandate of Heaven was
     a. a law code written by the Shang emperors
     b. the instructions for ritual sacrifice in Shang China
     c. invoked by the Chou to justify conquering the Shang
     d. the collection of pronouncements attributed to the "Deity Above"

24. The Olmecs
     a. built pyramids in the Andes
     b. cultivated maize in the North American Southwest
     c. flourished along the northern coast of Peru
     d. were the earliest Mesoamerican civilization

25. Events in Egyptian history are traditionally dated by reference to
     a. the reign of royal dynasties
     b. the reign of particular kings
     c. the Egyptian creation myth
     d. the reign of the first king

When?

1. When did the earliest civilizations arise in Mesopotamia?

2. The Hyksos invasion occurred during which period of Egyptian history?

3. How long did the Assyrian Empire last after the conquest of Palestine-Syria?

4. When did the Aryans invade the Indus valley?

5. When did city-states arise in China compared to Mesopotamia?

Where?

Using the map on page 14 of your textbook, name the civilizations in which these cities or geographical features are located.

1. Ur   _____

2. Thebes   _____

3. Tigris River   _____

4. Assur   _____

5. Nile River   _____

6. Taurus Mountains   _____

7. Memphis   _____

8. Nineveh   _____

9. Babylon   _____

10. Ur   _____

How and Why?

1.   What was the Neolithic Revolution? What impact did it have upon the development of early civilization?

2. How did the Eastern Chou civilization differ from the Western Chou? In what specific ways were the Chou civilizations different from the Shang?

3. Compare and contrast the Mesopotamian and Egyptian civilizations. Explain the major aspects of their respective civilizations that brought about these differences.

4. Why is little known about the early Indus River valley civilization in relation to other major civilizations of the ancient world? What explanations can you give for the failure of the Indus civilization?

5. How did the Neolithic period in the Americas differ from that of other early civilizations?

Map Labeling

Identify these four civilizations and the rivers that helped nurture them on the map on page 14 of your textbook and place them on the map provided.

1. Mesopotamia and Babylonia
2. Tigris River
3. Euphrates River
4. Nile River

5. Assyria
6. Sumer
7. Nubia
8. Egypt

Draw and label the borders of the following empires using the map on page 14 of your textbook.

9. Hittite
10. Egypt

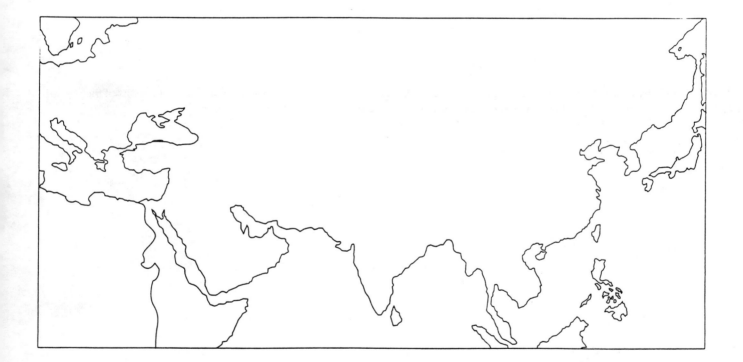

MULTIPLE CHOICE ANSWER KEY *(with page references)*

1. B (6)	11. A (9)	21. D (13)
2. D (7)	12. A (11)	22. B (18)
3. A (7)	13. B (12)	23. C (20)
4. B (8)	14. C (13)	24. D (22)
5. A (15)	15. B (19)	25. A (11)
6. C (11)	16. D (19)	
7. A (9)	17. D (21)	
8. B (9)	18. B (21)	
9. D (9)	19. D (22)	
10. D (8)	20. C (12)	

Chapter Two
The Four Great Revolutions in Thought and Religion

Practice Test

1. Which religious or philosophical revolution showed the greatest continuity of development over the centuries?
   - a. Chinese philosophy
   - b. Indian religion
   - c. Judaic monotheism
   - d. Greek philosophy

2. Why did the four religious or philosophical revolutions occur in areas of the original river-valley civilizations?
   - a. they were relatively isolated from attack
   - b. they were protected by geographical barriers
   - c. these areas contained agriculture, cities, literacy, and specialized professions
   - d. all of the above

3. According to Confucius, good government depended on
   - a. harsh, strictly enforced laws
   - b. the consent of the people
   - c. the appointment to office of good men
   - d. a strong military

4. In the Chinese worldview,
   - a. there is a distinct difference between this world and a supernatural world
   - b. there is no distinction between this world and a supernatural world
   - c. humans regulate the cosmological forces of heaven and earth
   - d. both b and c

5. Mencius believed
   - a. all men were basically good
   - b. all men were basically evil
   - c. the ultimate goal of human existence was the afterlife
   - d. both b and c

6. In his philosophical writings, Confucius advocated
   - a. social mobility and democratic government
   - b. an unbroken social harmony based on an understanding of one's place and responsibility in the social order
   - c. a realization that human nature was essentially bad and that it must be restrained
   - d. a freedom from the burden of social responsibilities

7. Taoism offers
   - a. a way of attaining power in a society dominated by social constraints
   - b. a refuge from the burden of social responsibilities
   - c. no political philosophy
   - d. a way to use knowledge in order to create social distinctions

8. Which of the following is a basic tenet of Taoism?
   - a. an action pushed to the extreme results in progress
   - b. too much government, even good government, can become oppressive
   - c. political democracy is the result of social responsibility
   - d. true peace requires a strong political state

9. In the Upanishadic worldview,
   a. knowledge is the ultimate source of power
   b. immortality is an escape from all existence
   c. immortality is found in an afterlife
   d. both a and b

10. The best definition of *samsara* is the
    a. endless cycle of renewed existence
    b. release from existence
    c. "right order of things"
    d. realization of one's fate

11. The paramount ideal for the Jains was the concept of
    a. *ahimsa*, or "noninjury"
    b. *samsara,* or "transmigration of the soul"
    c. *karma*, or "action"
    d. none of the above

12. Buddhism originated in
    a. India   c. Japan
    b. China   d. Nepal

13. The primary figure in the Buddhist religious tradition is
    a. Mahavira   c. Siddhartha Gautama
    b. Kshatriya   d. Dukkha

14. Abraham originally came from
    a. India
    b. Egypt
    c. Israel
    d. Mesopotamia

15. Which of the following Greek philosophers believed that the *polis* made individuals self-sufficient?
    a. Plato   c. Aristotle
    b. Thales   d. Anaxagoras

16. Yahweh refers to
    a. the Hebrew concept of the afterlife
    b. the Hebrew name for God
    c. a book of the Hebrew Bible
    d. the Israelite king

17. In Hebrew monotheism, the term prophet refers to
    a. one who enforces Torah
    b. the Israelite king
    c. a priest
    d. an inspired messenger from God

18. Hebrew religion influenced which later religion?
    a. Christianity
    b. Islam
    c. Judaism
    d. all of the above

19. The term exile refers to
    a. the flight of the Israelites from Egypt
    b. Abraham leaving Ur
    c. the captivity of Jews in Babylon after the fall of Israel
    d. the Hindu concept of afterlife

20. Greek philosophy is best described as
    a. rationalistic and skeptical
    b. reverent and mystical
    c. practical and simple
    d. both a and b

21. The Greek term logos means
    a. word
    b. language
    c. reason
    d. all of the above

22. The Greek term polis refers to
    a. a philosophical school
    b. a city-state
    c. an empire
    d. a household

23. Plato was
    a. a critic of Socrates
    b. an Ionian philosopher
    c. a student of Socrates
    d. a student of Aristotle

24. Which of the following religions did not develop in India?
    a. Judaism
    b. Jainism
    c. Hinduism
    d. Buddhism

25. The Buddhist teaching about the "Middle Path"
    a. required strict asceticism
    b. is the core of Buddhist faith and practice
    c. allowed for unrestricted self-indulgence
    d. both a and b

When

Comparing the chronologies throughout the chapter, in which centuries were the most important philosophers and religious figures active?

Where

Study Map 2-1 on page 35 of the textbook. Why did the cities of Jericho, Jerusalem, Hebron, and Beersheba continue to prosper throughout the ancient world? Why was the river Jordan so important in Biblical times?

How and Why

1. What do the four major philosophical and religious revolutions have in common in their development and impact on world history? Why are there so few religious and philosophical revolutions in history? Where did the major revolutions spread during the ancient time period?

2. What are the basic tenets of Confucian thought? How did they evolve and influence Chinese education? In what manner was Confucian thought different from other major religious and philosophical ideas?

3. Develop the central concept of the Tao, or the Way. Contrast this philosophical system with Confucianism and the impact on individuals in China. In what manner were there similar developments in other areas of the world?

4.   Explain the two basic tenets of the Nature of Reality in the Upanishadic worldview. How was this a fundamental change from the older Vedic concepts? What is the Upanishadic belief regarding the existence of an afterlife?

5.   What are the major aspects of Buddhist and Jain rebellion against Hinduism? Develop the proper historic background and time frame in your response. Why did Buddhism spread from India? In what ways are these religious movements similar and different?

6.   Describe the importance of the *Old Testament* as a reliable historic source. What is the importance of a written source for a religious belief? How is the *Old Testament* different from other revealed religious texts?

MAP LABELING

Identify these places and features of ancient Palestine on Map 2-1 on page 35 of your textbook and place them on the map provided.

1. Dead Sea

2. Sea of Galilee

3. Judah

4. Israel

5. Phoenicia

6. Gaza

7. Jerusalem

8. Jericho

9. Bethlehem

10. Sidon

11. Jordan River

12. Damascus

13. Megiddo

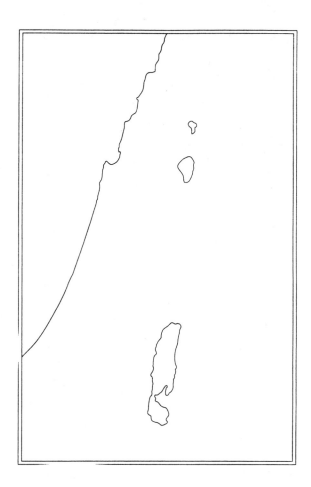

MULTIPLE CHOICE ANSWER KEY *(with page references)*

1. A (27)	11. A (32)	21 D (38)
2. C (26)	12. A (33)	22. B (39)
3. C (28)	13. C (33)	23. C (40)
4. D (27)	14. D (34)	24. A (32)
5. A (28)	15. C (41)	25. D (33)
6. B (27)	16. B (34)	
7. B (28)	17. D (35)	
8. B (29)	18. D (36)	
9. D (30)	19. C (35)	
10. A (31)	20. A (37)	

Chapter Three
Greek and Hellenistic Civilization

Practice Tests

1. The Minoan civilization was based on the
   a. island of Crete   c. mainland of Greece
   b. island of Thera   d. coast of Ionia

2. Which of the following is in the correct chronological order?
   a. Minoan period, Mycenaean period, Middle Age, sack of Troy
   b. Mycenaean period, Minoan period, sack of Troy, Middle Age
   c. Minoan period, Mycenaean period, sack of Troy, Middle Age
   d. sack of Troy, Middle Age, Minoan period, Mycenaean period

3. The highest virtue of a Homeric hero was
   a. speed of foot   c. *arete,* or courage
   b. *agon*, or desire   d. moral simplicity

4. Tyrants often came to power as a result of
   a. an assassination of a political leader
   b. a military defeat
   c. a peasant rebellion
   d. their military ability and support of the hoplites

5. Which of the following was a legacy of tyrants during the period 700-500 B.C.E.?
   a. they temporarily put an end to civil wars
   b. they reduced warfare among states
   c. they encouraged progressive economic changes
   d. all of the above

6. Which of the following was the location of the great Athenian victory against the Persians in 490 B.C.E.?
   a. Marathon   c. Salamis
   b. Boeotia   d. Thermopylae

7. The Delian League was transformed into the Athenian Empire because
   a. of the pressure of war against Persia
   b. of the rebellions of the Athenian allies
   c. the allies were unwilling to see to their own defenses
   d. all of the above

8. Women in Athens
   a. enjoyed full voting privileges
   b. were welcomed as important contributors to Athenian society and political life
   c. were excluded from most aspects of public life
   d. both a and b

9. The Athenian strategy during the opening phase of the Great Peloponnesian War was to
   a. allow the devastation of their land and rely on the income from their empire
   b. meet the Spartan army in battle
   c. force their allies to fight Sparta in pitched battle
   d. all of the above

10. The Sicilian expedition of 413 B.C.E. resulted in
    a. the rise to power of Alcibiades
    b. an Athenian victory
    c. the destruction of the entire Athenian force
    d. a Spartan alliance with Persia

11. Place these in the correct chronological order:
    a. Great Peloponnesian War, Spartan hegemony, Theban hegemony, rise of Macedon
    b. Spartan hegemony, Great Peloponnesian War, Theban hegemony, rise of Macedon
    c. Theban hegemony, Spartan hegemony, rise of Macedon, Great Peloponnesian War
    d. Great Peloponnesian War, Theban hegemony, Spartan hegemony, rise of Macedon

12. Macedon was
    a. a polis   c. an island in the Aegean
    b. a Greek-speaking kingdom   d. a member of the Delian League

13. In 338 B.C.E., Philip ended Greek autonomy at the battle of
    a. Thermopylae   c. Marathon
    b. Athens   d. Chaeronea

14. After the death of Alexander in 323 B.C.E., his entire empire
    a. passed to the control of Ptolemy
    b. passed to the control of Seleucus
    c. broke apart into smaller parcels
    d. was conquered by the Medes

15. The Stoics
    a. sought the happiness of the individual
    b. believed that everyone had a spark of divinity in him or her
    c. were determined to lead the virtuous life
    d. all of the above

16. Mycenaean people
    a. were warriors led by a strong king
    b. lived on the island of Crete
    c. were conquered by the Minoans
    d. lived in cities that lacked fortifications

17. Homeric society was
    a. democratic
    b. egalitarian
    c. aristocratic
    d. peaceful

18. The hoplite phalanx was
    a. an individual Greek champion
    b. an infantry formation
    c. the basic unit of Greek warfare
    d. both b and c

19. Magna Graecia refers to
    a. the Aegean Sea
    b. Ionia
    c. Southern Italy and Sicily
    d. Athens and Sparta

20. The symposion
     a. was a center for aristocratic social life
     b. included games and entertainment
     c. was a drinking party
     d. all of the above

21. Spartan girls
     a. were permitted more freedom than among other Greeks
     b. were permitted less freedom than among other Greeks
     c. fought in the army
     d. were considered property

22. Sparta was governed by
     a. a king
     b. a king, a council of elders, and an assembly
     c. a council of elders and an assembly
     d. a king and a council of elders

23. The word that best describes Greek life, thought, art, and literature in the classical period is
     a. serenity
     b. tension
     c. calm
     d. underdeveloped

24. The first person to write a prose history was
     a. Herodotus
     b. Hesiod
     c. Homer
     d. Thucydides

25. Alexandria was
     a. a Hellenistic mathematician
     b. one of Alexander's daughters
     c. the literary center of the Hellenistic world
     d. the capital of Macedon

When

1. During which period of Greek history did Homer live?

2. Did tyrants reign in Athens before or after the reforms of Clisthenes?

3. About how long did the Persian Wars last?

4. From the formation of the Delian League to Athen's defeat in the Peloponnesian War, how long did the Athenian Empire last?

5. How many years did it take Alexander to conquer the Persian Empire?

Where

1. Using Map 3-1 on page 55 of your textbook fill in the blanks below.

a. the northernmost Greek colony   _____

b. the westernmost Greek colony   _____

c. the westernmost Phoenician colony   _____

d. the southernmost Greek colony   _____

2. Based on Map 3-2 on page 62 of your textbook, what would you say is the most important form of transportation in the Greek world?

3. Compare Map 3-1 on page 55 with Map 3-3 on page 69 of the textbook. Specifically, where and how did Alexander expand Greek influence beyond the Mediterranean? Do you think it valid that Alexander is often referred to as having "conquered the world"?

How and Why

1.   Who were the Minoans and Mycenaeans? What kinds of evidence about their civilizations do we possess? What was the relationship of Mycenaean to Minoan culture? Why did the Mycenaean civilization fail?

2.   Compare and contrast the fundamental political, social, and economic institutions of Athens and Sparta, about 500 B.C.E. What were the major differences? Similarities?

3.   Describe the workings of the system of government that Clisthenes created. What were its main features? What were the main changes from the previous system? What did the system mean to the common citizen?

4.   Explain how the Athenian empire came into existence. Did it offer any advantages to its members? To what extent was the empire the basis for Athenian achievement in the fifth century and the basis for Athenian decline?

5.   What were the major consequences of Alexander's death? Why did his empire fail to maintain political unity? Assess the achievement of Alexander.

Map Labeling

Identify the following locations on Map 3-2 on page 62 of your textbook and place them on the map provided.

1. Aegean Sea

2. Ionian Sea

3. Mediterranean Sea

4. Crete

5. Asia Minor

6. Macedonia

7. Athens

8. Sparta

9. Corinth

10. Delphi

11. Olympia

12. Megara

13. Argos

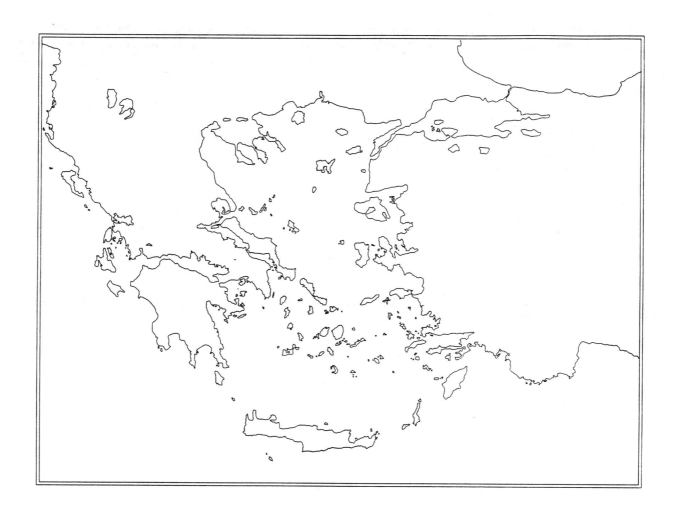

MULTIPLE CHOICE ANSWER KEY *(with page references)*

1. A (50)	11. A (65)	21. A (58)
2. C (56)	12. B (67)	22. B (58)
3. C (52)	13. D (67)	23. B (68)
4. D (54)	14. C (70)	24. A (69)
5. D (56)	15. D (71)	25. C (71)
6. A (60)	16. A (51)	
7. D (61)	17. C (52)	
8. C (63)	18. D (53)	
9. A (65)	19. C (54)	
10. C (65)	20. D (59)	

Chapter Four
Iran, India, and Inner Asia to 200 C.E.

Practice Test

1. The most prominent of the Iranian peoples were
   - a. Bactrians
   - b. Persians
   - c. Medes
   - d. both b and c

2. The emphasis of old Iranian religion was on
   - a. Shiva
   - b. "Lie"
   - c. "Truth" or "Right"
   - d. "the Tao" or "Way"

3. The first person to stand out in Iranian history was
   - a. Cyrus
   - b. Cambyses
   - c. Zarathustra
   - d. Darius

4. Zoroaster (628-551 B.C.E.) preached a message similar to all of the following except:
   - a. Hebrew prophets
   - b. Democritus
   - c. Buddha
   - d. Confucius

5. Zoroaster called on people to
   - a. abandon worship of Ahura Mazda
   - b. destroy the priestly clan known as the *Magi*
   - c. turn from the "Lie" (*druj*) to the "Truth" (*asha*)
   - d. all of the above

6. The greatest achievement of the Achaemenids was the
   - a. destruction of Pasargadae
   - b. relative stability of their rule
   - c. creation of the supreme deity Ahura Mazda
   - d. establishment of Zoroastrian ritual

7. A lasting contribution of the Kushan ruler, Kanishka, was the
   - a. school of Greco-Buddhist art in Gandhara
   - b. expulsion of the Achaemenids from India
   - c. destruction of magi influence at court
   - d. introduction of Hindu poetry to China

8. Much of the Achaemenid administrative success lay in their
   - a. tribal confederation
   - b. willingness to learn and borrow from predecessors
   - c. military despotism
   - d. forced conversion to the state religious cult

9. Chandragupta
   - a. defeated Alexander
   - b. supported Buddhism
   - c. created the first Indian empire
   - d. was the son of Ashoka

10. *Dharma* can best be defined as
    - a. nonviolence
    - b. "life-blood"
    - c. "conquest by righteousness"
    - d. "holy war"

11. Mauryan bureaucracy was marked by
    a. centralization   c. a secret service
    b. corruption   d. both a and c

12. Two masterpieces of Sanskrit culture around 200 C.E. were
    a. *Shiva* and *Vishnu*   c. *Arthashastra* and *Shahanshah*
    b. *Mahabharata* and *Ramayana*   d. *Asha* and *Gathas*

13. A primary reason that Buddhism remained only one among many Indian religious paths was
    a. that it was absorbed into the diversity that typifies the Hindu religious scene
    b. the fact most people could not read the Buddhist religious tracts
    c. that Buddhist saints were never identified with popular Indian deities
    d. that lay people could not spend the time trying to attain *nirvana* as could Buddhist monks

14. Culturally, the Parthians were oriented toward the Hellenistic world until the mid-first century C.E. when they were influenced by
    a. Iranian art motifs   c. the Greek alphabet
    b. Roman statuary   d. commerce with China

15. In the first century B.C.E. the Sakas were defeated in northwestern India by the
    a. Yueh Chih from the steppes of China   c. Jaxartes and his pirate raiders
    b. Bactrian Greeks from the west   d. *Pahlavas* invading from Iran

16. The ruler of the Achaemenid Empire was called
    a. satrap
    b. Ahura mazda
    c. shahanshah
    d. Seleucus

17. Ashoka underwent a religious conversion to
    a. Buddhism
    b. Hinduism
    c. Zoroastrianism
    d. none of the above

18. In the post-Mauryan period (200-300 C.E.), North India was dominated by
    a. Alexander's successors
    b. a Persian satrap
    c. an influx of various foreign people
    d. cultural isolation

19. The Greek general Seleucus
    a. established an Indo-Bactrian state
    b. ruled most of the former Achaemenid Empire
    c. ruled most of the former Mauryan Empire
    d. defeated the Kushans

20. The farthest reach of Hellenization in the East came under
    a. the Kushans
    b. the Seleucids
    c. the Sakas
    d. the Indo-Greeks

21. The magi were
    a. Zoroastrian priests
    b. Persian governors
    c. Hindu priests
    d. Parthian warriors

22. The Achaemenids
    a. imposed their traditions on conquered peoples
    b. spread Greek culture
    c. scattered conquered ethnic groups
    d. tolerated the traditions of conquered peoples

23. One of the greatest achievements in post-Mauryan India (200-300 C.E.) was
    a. the spread of Zoroastrianism
    b. the Gandharan school of art
    c. the conquest of southern India
    d. the development of Buddhism

24. One result of the Achaemenid conquest of Iran and Mesopotamia was
    a. the beginning of the Babylonian exile of the Jews
    b. the destruction of the Jewish Temple
    c. the end of the Babylonian exile of the Jews
    d. both a and b

25. Which Mauryan king provided a model of the ideal king in later Hindu and Buddhist thought?
    a. Ashoka
    b. Chandragupta
    c. Bindusara
    d. Kalinga

When

1. How long was Achmaenid rule of Iran compared to Seleucid rule?

2. How long after Alexander's campaigns in the Indus valley did the Mauryan Empire rise?

3. Which empire succeeded the Seleucids in Iran?

4. Based on the chronologies throughout the chapter, what was the significance of Alexander's campaigns in Indian, Iranian, and inner Asian history?

Where

1. Compare the extent of the Persian Empire as depicted in Map 4-1 on page 78 of the textbook with Alexander's Empire (Map 3-3, page 69) and the Roman Empire (Map 5-1, page 106). List these empires in chronological order. What similarities and differences do you see in the borders and extent of these empires?

2. Using Map 4-2 on page 81 of your textbook, identify the following cities as belonging to either the Seleucid, Indo-Greek, or Mauryan regions.

a. Ekbatana   _____

b. Ujjain   _____

c. Persepolis   _____

d. Sanchi   _____

e. Qandahar   _____

How and Why

1.   Why was Ashoka's conversion to Buddhism important in the creation of the Mauryan Empire? What were some of the policies effected by Ashoka? Discuss the Mauryan legacy in world history.

2. How did the Achaemenid state rule over a long period of time? What were the main aspects of government control that enhanced the power base? What was the role of religion in this development?

3. Discuss the major features of the Hindu and Buddhist traditions. What are the similarities between the two groups? Why did Buddhism spread to China and southeast Asia while Hinduism remained in India?

4. Describe the effect Hellenistic culture had on the Seleucid rule. How were its concepts different from those of Alexander the Great? What were the major contributions of the Greek world to the East and what was the specific effect on Bactria?

5. What major role did the steppe people play in the Eurasian subcontinent? How did the Parthians control a vast area with only a limited culture? What were the major differences between the rule of the Sakas and Kushans and the rule of the Parthians? In what ways can the Kushans and Sakas be considered important to world history?

MAP LABELING

The Achaemenid Empire touched all of these bodies of water. Locate them on the map on page 78 of your textbook and copy them onto the map provided.

1. Black Sea

2. Caspian Sea

3. Aral Sea

4. Persian Gulf

5. Red Sea

6. Mediterranean Sea

7. Aegean Sea

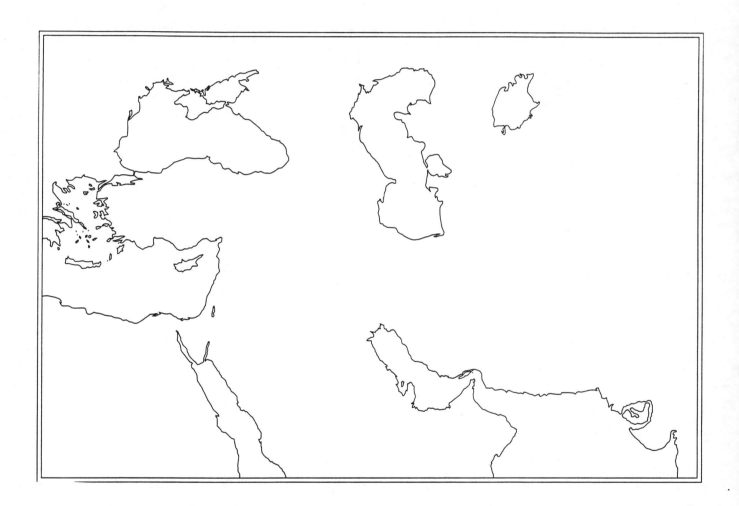

MULTIPLE CHOICE ANSWER KEY *(with page references)*

1. D (76)	11. D (82)	21. A (77)
2. C (77)	12. B (85)	22. D (79)
3. C (77)	13. A (85)	23. B (84)
4. B (77)	14. A (87)	24. C (78)
5. C (77)	15. D (87)	25. A (82)
6. B (79)	16. C (79)	
7. A (88)	17. A (82)	
8. B (79)	18. C (84)	
9. C (81)	19. B (85)	
10. C (82)	20. D (86)	

Chapter Five
Republican and Imperial Rome

Practice Test

1. *Imperium* can best be defined as the
   a. right to issue and enforce commands
   b. right to collect taxes
   c. right of property
   d. none of the above

2. A Roman woman
   a. could be sold or killed by her husband
   b. enjoyed a respected position in the family and ran the household
   c. was the chief priest of the family
   d. could vote in the assembly

3. In Rome, the patron-client relationship was
   a. based on fear of one for the other
   b. based on heredity
   c. sanctioned by religion and custom
   d. both b and c

4. The Roman constitution was
   a. an unwritten accumulation of laws and customs
   b. a written document kept under the strictest security
   c. a compiled record of several Italian constitutions
   d. both a and c

5. The Struggle of the Orders
   a. was a patrician campaign to achieve political, legal, and social equality
   b. resulted in the fall of the Roman Republic
   c. resulted in the decline of the Senate
   d. none of the above

6. The tribunate of Tiberius Gracchus proved that a Roman could
   a. pursue a political career that was not based solely on influence within the aristocracy
   b. appeal to the popular will of the people for influence
   c. no longer ignore the power of the senate
   d. both a and b

7. The First Triumvirate consisted of
   a. Pompey, Caesar, and Sulla
   b. Caesar, Crassus, and Marius
   c. Pompey, Caesar, and Crassus
   d. Marius, Sulla, and Pompey

8. Caesar established his fame as a general by
   a. defeating Spartacus   c. conquering Gaul
   b. destroying Octavian   d. saving Rome from Catiline

29

9. Augustus was successful in making the transition from a republican government because he
    a. emphasized his military power
    b. maintained the appearance of republican institutions and masked the monarchical reality
    c. eliminated all of his rivals
    d. emphasized his unprecedented powers and disregarded republican traditions

10. During his lifetime, Augustus
    a. accepted divine honors
    b. introduced foreign gods into the Roman cults
    c. repealed legislation curbing divorce and adultery
    d. none of the above

11. The poets Virgil and Horace were
    a. patronized by Augustus
    b. executed by Augustus
    c. mere propagandists
    d. exiled to the Black Sea region for displeasing Augustus

12. The peaceful accession of adoptive emperors ended
    a. with the assassination of Domitian
    b. when Marcus Aurelius' son, Commodus, ascended to the throne
    c. when Nerva chose the warlike Trajan as his successor
    d. when Caligula was assassinated

13. The main contribution of the Romans to architecture lay in
    a. their use of marble
    b. the great size of structures they could build because of engineering advancements
    c. their extreme attention to detail, especially in reducing the scale of buildings
    d. their attention to religious structures

14. The most serious persecution of Christians was instituted by
    a. Diocletian   c. the Jewish Pharisees
    b. Constantine   d. mobs

15. The Council of Nicea in 325,
    a. affirmed that Arianism was the accepted doctrine of the Christian Church
    b. sought to define the nature of the Trinity
    c. was called by the Emperor Constantine
    d. both b and c

16. The center of Roman life was
    a. the family
    b. the polis
    c. the individual
    d. the king

17. The end of the monarchy period
    a. decreased the power of the Senate
    b. increased the power of the plebeians
    c. increased the power of the Senate
    d. both a and b

18. Roman policy towards conquered peoples included
    a. full citizenship to cities close to Rome
    b. municipal status
    c. colonization
    d. all of the above

19. The Punic Wars extended Roman power into
    a. the Eastern Mediterranean
    b. Northern Europe
    c. the Western Mediterranean
    d. Asia

20. Roman education
    a. was the responsibility of the family
    b. was conducted by a system of public schools
    c. encouraged morality, piety, and respect for tradition
    d. both a and b

21. Jesus won a following especially among
    a. the Jewish elite
    b. the Roman elite
    c. poor people
    d. honestiores

22. Paul of Tarsus
    a. was a Roman citizen
    b. was a Pharisee
    c. converted to Christianity
    d. all of the above

23. The most important social distinction in third-century Rome was between
    a. Christians and pagans
    b. honestiores and humiliores
    c. senators and equestrians
    d. honestiores and equestrians

24. Diocletian instituted
    a. the tetrarchy
    b. the Council of Nicea
    c. the principate
    d. the Punic Wars

25. One of the main features of late Roman culture was
    a. the preservation of classical culture
    b. the closeness and complexity of pagan culture and Christianity
    c. the persecution of Christians
    d. both a and b

When

1. To what extent did the Punic Wars coincide with Roman expansion to the East?

2. What relationship do the chronologies on pages 97, 101, and 102 of your textbook, suggest between Roman expansion and the fall of the Republic?

3. How long was the average reign of the "Good Emperors"?

Where

Using Map 5-1 on page 106 of the textbook fill in the blank after each province with the letter that corresponds to the period when the province was conquered by Rome.

A. before 14 C.E.   B. 14 – 98 C.E.   C. 98-117 C.E.

1. Galatia_____

2. Rhaetia_____

3. Britain_____

4. Armenia_____

5. Africa_____

Compare the map 5-1 on page 106 of your textbook with map 5-2 on page 114 of your textbook. What impact did the support of the emperors have on the spread of Christianity?

How and Why

1. What was the "struggle of the orders"? What did the plebeians want? What methods did they use to get what they wanted? To what degree was Roman society different after the struggle ended?

2. Explain the causes of the clash between the Romans and the Carthaginians in the First and Second Punic Wars. Could the wars have been averted? Who bears the ultimate responsibility?

3. What domestic problems did Italy have in the middle of the second century B.C.E.? What caused these problems? What were the main proposals of Tiberius and Gaius Gracchus? Why did they fail? What other questions about Roman domestic policy had the Gracchi raised through their deaths?

4. Why was the Roman population willing to accept Augustus as head of the state? What answers did Augustus provide for the problems that had plagued the republic? Describe the Augustan settlement of government. In what manner did Augustus rule?

5.   Despite unpromising beginnings, Christianity was enormously successful by the fourth century C.E. What religions were its competitors? What were the more important reasons that help explain its success?

Map Labeling

By the time of Augustus' death, Roman domination had spread across the Mediterranean from Iberia to Asia and part of Africa. Identify the following locations on Map 5-1 on page 106 of your textbook and place them on the map provided on the next page.

1. Rome

2. Italy

3. Mauritania (client kingdom)

4. Thrace (client kingdom)

5. Palestine

6. Armenia

7. Gaul

8. Corsica

9. Sardinia

10. Sicily

11. Illyricum

12. Asia

13. Macedon

14. Cilicia

15. Cyprus

16. Crete

17. Achaea

18. Spain

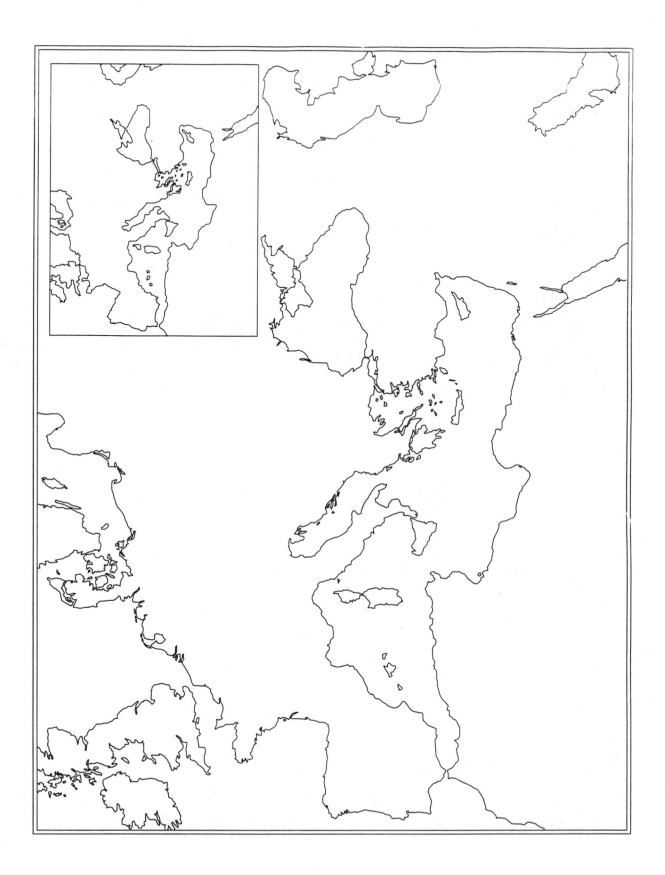

MULTIPLE CHOICE ANSWER KEY *(with page references)*

1. A (94)	11. A (104)	21. C (109)
2. B (94)	12. B (105)	22. D (109)
3. D (95)	13. B (107)	23. B (111)
4. A (95)	14. A (113)	24. A (112)
5. D (96)	15. D (115)	25. D (116)
6. D (100)	16. A (94)	
7. C (102)	17. C (95)	
8. C (102)	18. D (96)	
9. B (103)	19. C (97)	
10. D (102)	20. D (98)	

Chapter Six
Africa: Early History to 1000 C.E.

Practice Test

1. Which of the following is <u>not</u> a river in Africa?
    a. Orinoco   c. Orange
    b. Nile   d. Zambezi

2. In most of Africa, which of the following poses a perennial problem?
    a. water shortage
    b. lack of abundant animal life
    c. crop pests
    d. both a and c

3. Significant trading commodities in Africa included
    a. agricultural goods
    b. mineral resources
    c. silk
    d. manufactured goods

4. What was the result of the rapid desiccation of the Saharan region in the second millennium B.C.E.?
    a. population dispersal to the eastern Sahara
    b. population dispersal to the Sudanic regions
    c. invasion of the region by conquerors from the east
    d. the transition to bronze tools and weapons

5. By the tenth century B.C.E., Kush
    a. had conquered the Egyptian empire
    b. had emerged as a virtually independent kingdom
    c. had declined and was conquered by the Seleucids
    d. was attacked and conquered by the Egyptians

6. Which of the following represents the correct chronological order of empires in Nilotic Africa and the Ethiopian highlands?
    a. Meroitic empire, Napatan empire, Aksumite empire
    b. Napatan empire, Meroitic empire, Aksumite empire
    c. Aksumite empire, Meroitic empire, Napatan empire
    d. Napatan empire, Aksumite empire, Meroitic empire

7. In the sixth century B.C.E., which of the following had become the center of a flourishing iron industry?
    a. Napata   c. Meroe
    b. Aksum   d. Jenne

8. In the Meroitic empire, political succession
    a. was hereditary from father to son
    b. was often through the maternal rather than paternal line
    c. forbade the possibility of a woman monarch
    d. both a and c

9. The weakened Kushite empire was supplanted about 330 C.E. by
    a. Aksum   c. Nok
    b. Napata   d. Yemen

10. The Aksumite empire was controlled by
    a. a strong priestly class with ties to the eastern Orthodox church
    b. a king of kings through tribute-paying vassals
    c. a commercial oligarchy
    d. a ruling council with limited war making powers

11. Ethiopia
    a. was predominantly Muslim
    b. was predominantly Christian
    c. remained a center of trade after the fall of Aksum
    d. both a and c

12. In the African subcontinent, the vast majority of the peoples speak languages that belong to a single language group known as
    a. Khoisan
    b. Malagasy
    c. *Periplus*
    d. Bantu

13. Overseas trade with East Africa
    a. was more international than the earliest sources indicate
    b. was minimal at best
    c. extended north to Spain and France
    d. both a and c

14. The most important export from East Africa was
    a. slaves
    b. gold
    c. ivory
    d. spices

15. From a world perspective, Africa was
    a. engaged with overseas neighbors in extensive trading
    b. important because it was the home of Islam
    c. probably the location where the human species originated
    d. all of the above

16. The earliest iron age culture in Africa was the
    a. Nok
    b. Bantu
    c. Aksum
    d. Kush

17. The Napatan empire
    a. was dominated by New Kingdom Egypt
    b. was the true successor to Pharaonic Egypt
    c. encouraged the worship of local deities
    d. all of the above

18. Which of the following encouraged the formation of large political entities in the western Sudan?
    a. a substantial growth in population by the second century C.E.
    b. the adoption of Islam
    c. trade with Egypt and the Nilotic Sudan
    d. both a and c

19. Early urban centers in the western Sudan
    a. developed in oasis or river regions
    b. developed along trade routes
    c. grew from religious centers
    d. all of the above

20. In the early Christian era, trans-Saharan trade was
    a. made difficult because of religious conflicts
    b. made more viable by the spread of Christianity
    c. made more viable by the introduction of domesticated camels
    d. made difficult by Roman dominance in North Africa

21. Which of the following items were import items imported to Africa
    a. pottery
    b. porcelain
    c. cotton
    d. all of the above

22. Africa
    a. has many natural harbors
    b. makes up over one-fifth of the Earth's landmass
    c. is unusually cold
    d. is poor in mineral resources

23. The interior and southern reaches of Africa
    a. were isolated from direct contact with Eurasia
    b. were in direct contact with Eurasia
    c. did not participate in international trade
    d. both a and c

24. During the first millennium B.C.E. the Sudanic peoples
    a. unified Africa north of the Sahara
    b. unified Africa south of the Sahara
    c. developed settled agriculture
    d. remained hunter-gatherers

25. After Pharaonic Egypt, the earliest known literate and politically unified civilization in Africa was
    a. the kingdom of Aksum
    b. the kingdom of Kush
    c. Ethiopia
    d. Kanem

When

1. When did the first known culture outside of Nilotic Africa flourish?

2. When did Latin and Greek writers first become aware of Aksum?

3. How precise is our chronology of the kingdoms of the western and central Sudan?

4. When did East Africa become linked to Indian Ocean trade?

Where

Study Map 6-2 on page 129 of your textbook. Identify the most important trading centers. Why did you make your particular selections? What does this map tell you about the trading activity of the western and central Sudan?

How and Why

1.   How would you describe the African continent from a physical perspective? What are the most important rivers, deserts, and climate zones? How has its physical geography, including mineral wealth, soil, water supply, and other natural factors affected the development of societies in Africa?

2.   What were some of the results of the desiccation of the Sahara region after 2500 B.C.E.? What effect did this process have on the distribution of peoples, pottery, and agriculture techniques?

3.   Who were the Nok people and why are they important in the study of the early Iron Age in Africa?

4.   Discuss the transfer of power from the Napatan empire to the Meroitic empire. What are the specific reasons for the Napatan fall and why was Meroitic Kush able to succeed? In the same manner, discuss the fall of the Meroitic empire and the rise of Aksum. What general statements about the causes of political transition can you make after this analysis?

Map Labeling

Look carefully at Map 6-1 on page 125 of the textbook. Familiarize yourself with the names of regions and cultures that form the basis of this chapter. Identify the following sites and features of ancient Africa on Map 6-1 reproduced on the next page:

1. Bantu migrations
2. Spread of Iron Smelting
3. Maqurra
4. Napata
5. Jenne
6. Kush

7. Egypt
8. Nubia
9. Abyssinia (Ethiopia)
10. Indian Ocean
11. Kalahari Desert
12. Lake Victoria

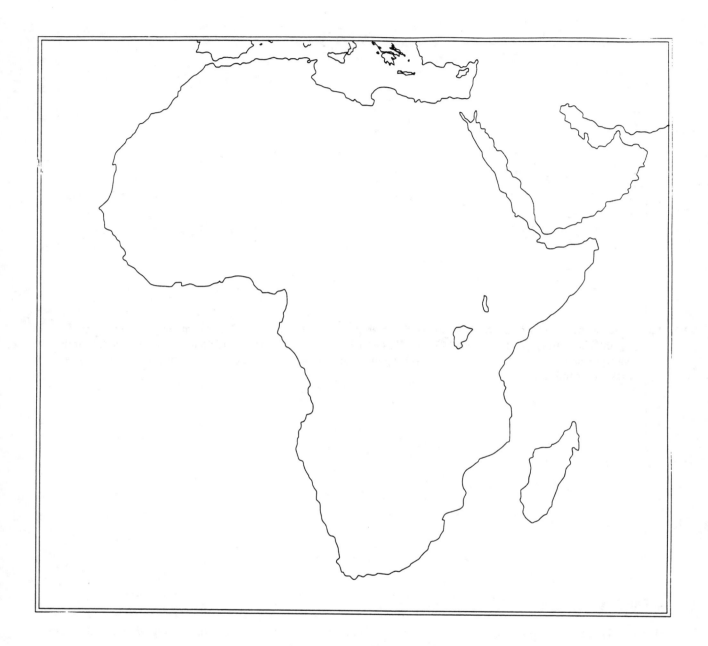

MULTIPLE CHOICE ANSWER KEY *(with page references)*

1. A (120)
2. D (120)
3. B (120)
4. B (121)
5. B (124)
6. B (126)
7. C (124)
8. B (126)
9. A (127)
10. B (127)

11. B (128)
12. D (131)
13. A (132)
14. C (132)
15. D (134)
16. A (123)
17. B (124)
18. D (128)
19. A (129)
20. C (130)

21. D (133)
22. B (120)
23. A (121)
24. C (123)
25. B (124)

Chapter Seven
China's First Empire (221 B.C.E. - 220 C.E.)

Practice Test

1. China was unified by the
   - a. Ch'in dynasty
   - b. Former Han dynasty
   - c. Later Han dynasty
   - d. Chou dynasty

2. The Ch'in state was located on the
   - a. Yellow River
   - b. Huai River
   - c. Wei River
   - d. Yangtze River

3. The Great Wall of China was built to
   - a. consolidate the diverse peoples under Ch'in rule
   - b. protect against the incursion of aggressive tribes from the north
   - c. split the Ch'in and Chou kingdoms
   - d. establish clear boundaries between prefectures

4. After the death of the First Emperor in 210 B.C.E., the Ch'in dynasty
   - a. was destroyed by the domino effect of its own legal codes
   - b. maintained its organization under the rule of Wang Mang
   - c. was destroyed under pressure by the Yellow Turbans
   - d. both a and c

5. The "dynastic cycle" begins with
   - a. internal wars
   - b. economic growth
   - c. strong centralized political authority
   - d. both b and c

6. In the "Salt and Iron Debate," Confucian scholars argued that
   - a. the state should enjoy the profits from the sale of salt and iron
   - b. salt and iron should be left in private ownership
   - c. the government should expand its territory in search of resources
   - d. Japan should be allowed to join the search for resources in China

7. The Former Han dynasty
   - a. reduced the centralized bureaucracy
   - b. relied on a Legalist administrative structure
   - c. continued the centralized bureaucratic administration of the Ch'in
   - d. both b and c

8. The "son of heaven" was a title that provided
   - a. justification for republican rule
   - b. complete power for the empress dowager
   - c. an ethical justification for dynastic rule
   - d. none of the above

9. The pilgrimage of the Tang monk, Hsuan Tsang, was novelized as
   - a. *Journey to Karma*
   - b. *The Yellow Turban*
   - c. *Journey to the West*
   - d. *The Red Eyebrows*

10. On the death of the emperor Kao Tsu in 195 B.C.E., China was
    a. overrun by the Hsiung Nu
    b. controlled by the Empress Lu
    c. ruled by Wang Mang
    d. none of the above

11. Neo-Taoism was concerned with
    a. achieving Nirvana
    b. "focused learning"
    c. immortality
    d. both a and b

12. *Tale of the Three Kingdoms* was a
    a. compilation of military stories
    b. nationalistic piece of propaganda
    c. Confucian history
    d. great romantic epic of Chinese literature

13. Han philosophy
    a. has been criticized for having a mechanistic view of nature
    b. tries to encompass the interrelationships of the natural world
    c. spurred advances in astronomy, music, and medicine
    d. all of the above

14. Ssu-Ma Ch'ien was famous for his
    a. Neo-Taoist philosophy
    b. history of the known world
    c. *Spring and Autumn Annals*
    d. both b and c

15. Which of the following was an advantage that Buddhism had over Taoism in the competition between the two religions?
    a. Buddhism offered no concept of an afterlife
    b. Buddhism contained high standards of personal ethics
    c. Buddhism rejected the complex Indian tradition of meditative practices
    d. Buddhism was never persecuted

16. The First Emperor of the Ch'in
    a. ruled according to Legalist precepts
    b. ruled according to Confucian precepts
    c. introduced Buddhism to China
    d. maintained the Chou system of rule

17. Wu Ti
    a. established government monopolies on items such as salt, copper, and iron
    b. built a canal linking the economic centers of North China
    c. aggressively expanded the borders
    d. all of the above

18. The Han dynasty
    a. maintained the Legalist structure of government left by the Ch'in
    b. replaced the Legalist structure of government with a Confucian system
    c. Confucianized the Legalist structure of government
    d. imitated Roman models of government

19. Wang Mang
      a. was the first Chinese empress
      b. was the regent to an infant emperor until starting his own dynasty
      c. restored the Han dynasty after a revolt
      d. moved the capital to Loyang

20. In the north, state formation depended on
      a. the interaction of nomads and Chinese
      b. Indian Ocean trade
      c. the emergence of Nanking as a center of commerce
      d. the spread of Buddhism

21. Han philosophers and scholars
      a. compiled the first Chinese dictionary
      b. rejected Confucianism
      c. wrote commentaries on literary classics
      D. both a and c

22. Neo-Taoism
      a. appealed only to scholars
      b. included both elite and popular versions
      b. was the official philosophy of the Han
      d. both b and c

23. Buddhism spread rapidly through China in the third century B.C.E.
      a. during the collapse of the Han socio-political order
      b. through the support of royal courts
      c. due to conquest by Buddhist nomads
      d. both a and b

24. Chinese Buddhism
      a. adhered strictly to Indian Buddhism
      b. rejected ancestor worship
      c. differed from Indian Buddhism in many ways
      d. both a and b

25. The principal threat to the Han empire was
      a. the Hsiung Nu empire to the north
      b. Japan
      c. Confucian scholars
      d. the Mauryan empire in India

Where

1. Examine Map 7-2 on page 143 of your textbook. What is the relationship between Han expansion and trade?

2. Based on both Map 7-2 on page 143 and Map 7-3 on page 151 of your textbook, in what ways was Ch'ang-an an important city?

3. Examine Map 7-3 on page 151 of your textbook. By what routes did Buddhism spread into China?

How and Why

1.   What were the major reasons for the success of the expansion of the Ch'in empire? What were the geographic limits of the empire? Why was the Great Wall built and to what extent did it achieve its major purpose? How did the bureaucracy function?

2.   How did the Former Han rulers continue the policies of the Ch'in dynasty? How were they different? Why did the Silk Road come into existence in this time period?

3.   What was the "dynastic cycle" in China? Why was there a specific mandate from heaven for this political activity? What were the general reasons for a downward trend in the cycle?

4.   What were the contributions of philosophy to the Han dynasty? How did philosophy aid in uniting the large empire? What were some of the major controversies of the time?

5.   Why did Buddhism appeal to the Chinese? Why were some of the Indian practices utilized by many who became involved in the faith? What importance did the collapse of the Han dynasty have in this movement?

Map Labeling

This exercise will require you to use all three maps in the chapter (7-1, p. 139; 7-2, p. 143; 7-3, p. 151). After studying the three maps, draw the following features on the blank map on the following page.

1. Trace the borders of the Ch'in state with a solid line.
2. Trace the borders of the Han empire with a dotted line.
3. Use arrows to show the Silk Road.
4. Use dashes to trace the spread of Buddhism into China.
5. Identify Ch'ang-an.
6. Identify Loyang.

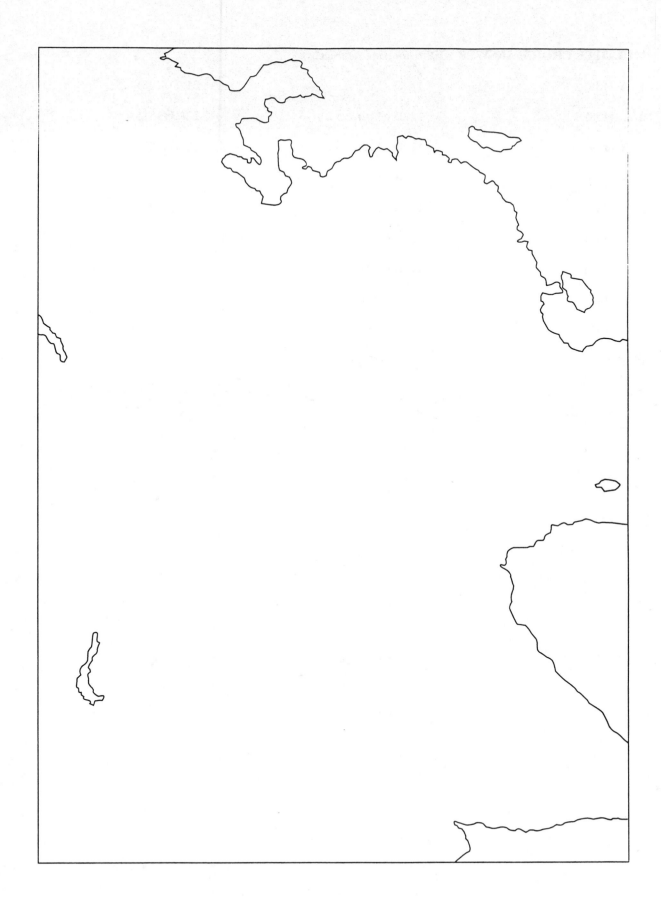

49

MULTIPLE CHOICE ANSWER KEY *(with page references)*

1. A (138)	11. C (150)	21. D (148)
2. C (138)	12. D (146)	22. B (151)
3. B (139)	13. D (149)	23. D (151)
4. A (140)	14. B (149)	24. C (152)
5. A (140)	15. B (151)	25. A (142)
6. B (142)	16. A (139)	
7. D (142)	17. D (142)	
8. C (144)	18. C (143)	
9. C (152)	19. B (145)	
10. B (144)	20. A (147)	

Chapter Eight
Imperial China (589-1368)

Practice Test

1. The most notable feature of Chinese history during the Sui and T'ang dynasties was the
   a. reunification of China
   b. disintegration of emperor worship
   c. recreation of a centralized bureaucratic empire
   d. both a and c

2. The throne in the Northern Wei was insecure and often usurped because the
   a. military was controlled by professional generals
   b. social distance between aristocracy and royalty was small
   c. state had no firm geographical barriers
   d. all of the above

3. During the reign of Sui Wen-ti, the Sui dynasty
   a. rebuilt the Great Wall
   b. built huge palaces
   c. restored the tax base
   d. all of the above

4. The Sui dynasty declined because
   a. the court became bankrupt and demoralized
   b. aggressive tribes invaded from Japan
   c. the loss of Chinese lives in wars with Korea produced discontent
   d. both a and c

5. The most important body in the T'ang administration was the
   a. Council of State
   b. Secretariat
   c. Censorate
   d. Chancellery

6. The equal field system
   a. was part of the Sui tax system
   b. was egalitarian for all able-bodied men
   c. gave special exemptions and advantages to the aristocracy
   d. both a and c

7. The Empress Wu Chao
   a. was a patron of the arts
   b. advocated state subsidies for poets
   c. murdered or exiled her rivals at court
   d. all of the above

8. After the Empress Wu Chao,
   a. the T'ang dynasty fell into political chaos
   b. no woman would ever become emperor again
   c. the Scholars of the North Gate were exiled
   d. the old northeastern Chinese aristocrats were exiled

9. The principal threats to the T'ang state were the
   a. Tibetans
   b. Turks
   c. Khitan Mongols
   d. all of the above

10. In their foreign relations, the T'ang dynasty
    a. refused to make allies
    b. generally conquered as many neighbors as possible
    c. employed a four-tier policy of defenses
    d. relied on the protection of Japan

11. Among the most important of achievements during the T'ang dynasty was the
    a. reform of the land system
    b. development of commercial contacts with neighboring countries
    c. consolidation of autonomous provinces
    d. destruction of renegade warlords

12. Which dynasty was associated with the Golden Age of Buddhism in China?
    a. Sui   c. Sung
    b. T'ang   d. Yuan

13. The millennium of late imperial China after the T'ang is often spoken of as the
    a. Age of Autocracy   c. Age of Imperialism
    b. Age of Absolute Monarchy d. both a and b

14. The Sung culture differed from that of the T'ang in that it became more
    a. intensely and narrowly Chinese
    b. expansive and inclusive of Japanese culture
    c. eclectic in nature
    d. none of the above

15. The greatest of Mongol leaders was
    a. Chang Chi-chih   c. Chu Hsi
    b. Genghis Kahn   d. Su Tung-p'o

16. T'ang culture was
    a. reactionary
    b. isolated
    c. cosmopolitan
    d. both a an b

17. Li Po is best described as
    a. Buddhist
    b. Taoist
    c. Legalist
    d. puritanical

18. After the fall of the T'ang
    a. the aristocracy declined
    b. the aristocracy filled the power vacuum
    c. many people were enslaved
    d. the equal field system maintained economic growth

19. From the late ninth century the center of gravity of China's population
    a. shifted to the Yellow River region
    b. shifted to the Yangtze region
    c. shifted west into conquered Tibetan lands
    d. lived in and around Ch'ang-an

20. Unlike Ch'ang-an, Sung capitals
     a. were highly organized within walls
     b. encouraged foreign residents
     c. were open within and spread beyond their outer walls
     d. both a and b

21. Unlike the earlier Arab expansion, Mongol conquests
     a. were aided by the unifying force of religious zeal
     b. were not aided by the unifying force of religious zeal
     c. were focused only on China
     d. both a and c

22. Kublai Khan
     a. ruled China from the Mongol capital of Karakorum
     b. adopted the dynastic name, Yuan
     c. ruled the Golden Horde
     d. made peace with the southern Sung

23. Mongol rule
     a. brought China into contact with other civilizations
     b. isolated China from the rest of the world
     c. expanded Chinese trade
     d. both a and c

24. The favored religion among the Mongols was
     a. Islam
     b. Chinese Buddhism
     c. Tibetan Buddhism
     d. Indian Buddhism

25. The Yuan dynasty
     a. was the shortest lived of China's major dynasties
     b. lasted for several centuries
     c. restored Confucian values
     d. is remembered as a Chinese Golden Age

Where

Using the Map 8-2 on page 170, fill in the blank after each term with the appropriate letter.

A. Remained part of Sung China   B. Lost to Ch'in   C. Never part of Sung China

1. Chengtu   _____

2. To-t'ung   _____

3. Hangchow   _____

4. Yen-ching   _____

5. Kaifeng   _____

How and Why

1. What is the importance of the Sui dynasty to the T'ang dynasty? What former Chinese empire developed a role model for these two dynasties? What great building program developed in the Sui period?

2. Why was Empress Wu (625-706) successful in obtaining control in the T'ang period? How did her role affect Chinese history? Did her influence enhance or detract from the prestige of the T'ang empire?

3. Describe how peasants in China changed from serfs to free farmers. What was the role of the aristocracy in this transformation? Why did the equal field system collapse?

4.   Discuss the influence of technological changes during the Sung period. What was the impact of money on trade? Why did the population shift to the south? What role did the scholar-gentry play in these changes?

5.   Describe the methods utilized by the Mongols to control China. What advantage was there in maintaining a language barrier between the Mongols and the Chinese? How did the "myriad system" work?

Map Labeling

The T'ang Empire reached its peak in the eighth century. Study Map 8-1 on page 159 of your textbook. On the map provided on the next page, shade in the area of the T'ang Empire and identify the following:

1. Ch'ang-an	6. Japan
2. Loyang	7. Nomadic Turkic Peoples
3. Yangtze River	8. Tarim Basin
4. Yellow River	9. Silla
5. Tibet	10. Kunlun Mountains

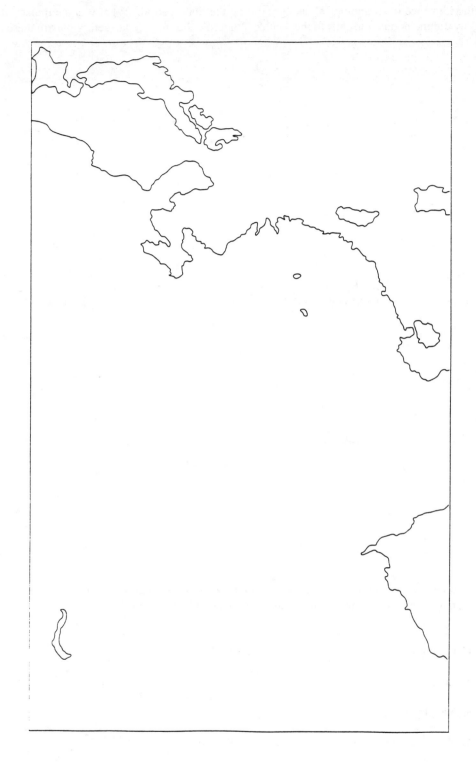

MULTIPLE CHOICE ANSWER KEY *(with page references)*

1. D (158)	11. A (164)	21. B (179)
2. B (158)	12. B (167)	22. B (180)
3. D (158)	13. D (173)	23. D (181)
4. D (158)	14. A (174)	24. B (183)
5. A (160)	15. B (178)	25. A (184)
6. C (160)	16. C (165)	
7. C (160)	17. B (168)	
8. B (160)	18. A (170)	
9. D (162)	19. B (171)	
10. C (162)	20. C (172)	

Chapter Nine
Japan: Early History to 1467

Practice Test

1. Each of the three main turning points in Japanese history was marked by
    a. the military defeat of Japanese armies
    b. a massive restructuring of Japanese institutions
    c. a major influx of an outside culture
    d. both b and c

2. The second phase of Japanese prehistory began about 300 B.C.E. with the
    a. Yayoi revolution
    b. Yamato state
    c. Jomon culture
    d. Tomb culture of the T'ang

3. By the first century the population in Japan had so expanded that
    a. Yayoi civilization collapsed
    b. Japan invaded Korea
    c. wars were fought over land
    d. a great famine broke out

4. The indigenous religion of Yamato Japan was an animistic worship of the forces of nature called
    a. *uji*
    b. *Shinto*
    c. *Kyushu*
    d. *Kamo*

5. Large scale institutional changes in Japanese government began in the 680s under the leadership of the
    a. Emperor Temmu
    b. Emperor Shirakawa
    c. Empress Jito
    d. both a and c

6. The emperors at the Nara and Heian courts were
    a. Confucian rulers
    b. Shinto rulers
    c. considered descendants of the sun goddess
    d. all of the above

7. The word *samurai* derives from a Japanese word meaning
    a. "to serve"
    b. "to fight"
    c. loyalty
    d. virtue

8. During the second half of the eleventh century Fujiwara rule gave way to control by
    a. military governors
    b. retired emperors
    c. specially appointed audit and police commissioners
    d. feuding *samurai* warriors

9. *Kana* was
    a. a syllabic script which was developed during the ninth century
    b. a series of Chinese characters that were used as phonetic symbols
    c. a Japanese concept expressing the idea of "Fate"
    d. none of the above

10. The world's first novel was
    a. *Ten Thousand Leaves*
    b. *The Tale of Genji*
    c. *Collection of Ancient and Modern Times*
    d. *The Pillow Book*

11. The two great Buddhist sects of the Heian era in Japan were
    a. Koya and Kana
    b. Sugawara and Michizane
    c. Yakushiji and Amaro
    d. Tendai and Shingon

12. The late twelfth century marked another major turning point in Japanese history because it
    a. began the shift from centuries of rule by a civil aristocracy to rule by the military
    b. saw the formation of the *bakufu*
    c. saw the emergence of the *shogun* as the de facto ruler of Japan
    d. all of the above

13. The invasion of Japan in 1281 by the Mongols was unsuccessful because
    a. Japanese tactics of fierce individual combat decimated the Mongol army
    b. the Kyoto court captured and beheaded Kublai Khan
    c. *kamikaze* sank a portion of the Mongol fleet
    d. both a and c

14. After the decline of Kamakura hegemony about 1335,
    a. Japan was finally conquered by the Mongols
    b. Ashikaga Takauji established a regional multistate system under the control of vassals
    c. power was transferred to the Nun Shogun
    d. Minamoto Yoritomo established his personal *bakufu*

15. An important aspect of Zen Buddhism was its
    a. influence on the arts of Japan
    b. emphasis on book learning and the "complex mind"
    c. lack of influence from China
    d. rejection of meditation and emphasis on interaction with the political world

16. The Records of Ancient matters and Records of Japan
    a. are the first novels in world history
    b. tell of the creation of Japan
    c. were composed by Buddhist monks
    d. imitate Chinese mythology

17. Yamato Japan
    a. was under constant threat of invasion from the mainland
    b. relied heavily on the use of eunuchs in government
    c. had no significant external enemies
    d. both a and b

18. Education at the Nara and Heian courts was largely a matter of
    a. studying Chinese literature and learning to write Chinese
    b. military training
    c. studying Japanese literature and learning Japanese
    d. both b and c

19. Minamoto Yoritomo referred to his government as
    a. the bakufu
    b. the shingon
    c. the shogun
    d. the kamikaze

20. The increase in Japanese population between 1200 C.E. and 1600 C.E. was brought about by
    a. land reclamation
    b. a cultural shift towards larger families
    c. improvements in agricultural technology
    d. both a and c

21. During the tenth and eleventh centuries itinerant preachers
        a. created a revival of Shintoism
        b. spread Pure Land Buddhism
        c. spread Zen Buddhism
        d. denounced the immorality of the court

22. Nichiren
        a. stressed a return to the "original mind"
        b. believed that a single invocation in praise of Amida was sufficient for salvation
        c. believed that the Lotus Sutra was the perfect embodiment of Buddha's teachings
        d. both a and b

23. No plays
        a. have no parallels in East Asian culture
        b. include both male and female performers
        c. use poetic language
        d. both a and c

24. The basic unit of Yamato aristocratic society was
        a. the immediate family
        b. the extended family
        c. the court
        d. the tribe

25. The Yamato were allies of
        a. Silla
        b. Koguryo
        c. Paechke
        d. Fujiwara

When

1. Although Japan has had an emperor for its entire history, often the emperor has been a figurehead. When in Japanese early history did emperors rule in fact?

2. Which military house governed Japan the longest? The shortest?

How and Why

1.   What were the major characteristics of earlier religions in Japan? How did Shintoism differ from Buddhism? In what manner was this development different from religions in China? Why was this movement confined to the islands of Japan?

2.   What was the agricultural system in use up to 838? Why did the "quota and estate" system come into existence?

3.   How did the Fujiwara clan rule from 856 to 1056? Why did the retired emperors gain control from this group? What was the importance of Kyoto as the political center from 710 to 1180?

4.   What were the important cultural contributions of the Nara and Heian periods in Japan? What was the first novel ever written and the impact of this book on the Japanese upper class?

5.   Why did the Mongol invasions of Japan fail? Where did the attacks take place? What was the Japanese main defense? What were the domestic political repercussions of these invasions on Japan?

Map Labeling

Identify the following features on Map 9-1 on page 190 of your textbook and place them on the map provided.

1. Korean Peninsula

2. Kyushu

3. Honshu

4. Shikoku

5. Silla

6. Paekche

7. Koguryo

8. Sea of Japan

9. East China Sea

10. Pacific Ocean

11. Yellow Sea

12. Nara

13. Heian (Kyoto)

MULTIPLE CHOICE ANSWER KEY *(with page references)*

1. D (188)	11. D (197)	21. B (201)
2. A (188)	12. D (198)	22. C (203)
3. C (188)	13. C (200)	23. D (204)
4. B (189)	14. B (200)	24. B (189)
5. D (191)	15. A (203)	25. C (189)
6. D (191)	16. C (190)	
7. A (193)	17. C (192)	
8. B (195)	18. A (195)	
9. A (196)	19. A (198)	
10. B (196)	20. D (201)	

Chapter Ten
Iran and India before Islam

Practice Test

1. The last century or so of Parthian rule saw increased emphasis on
    a. foreign traditions in religious and cultural affairs
    b. Iranian traditions in religious and cultural affairs
    c. Roman military techniques
    d. the wealth of Egypt to support its military needs

2. The Sassanids were a(n)
    a. Parthian dynasty
    b. Aramaic dynasty
    c. Persian dynasty
    d. Gupta dynasty

3. Shapur claimed to be "king of kings" based on his conquest of
    a. Bactria
    b. parts of the Roman Empire
    c. Syria, Armenia, and Anatolia
    d. all of the above

4. The greatest Sassanid emperor was
    a. Chosroes Anosharvan
    b. Ardashir
    c. Justinian the Wise
    d. Kirdir

5. Indian influences on the Sassanid civilization were especially evident in
    a. economic policies
    b. historical writing
    c. medicine and mathematics
    d. all of the above

6. Sassanid culture was drawn from the
    a. Roman tradition
    b. Hellenistic tradition
    c. Bactrian-Indian traditions
    d. all of the above

7. Kartir is important for his
    a. zealotry in support of Zoroastrian theology
    b. conversion to Manichaeism
    c. support of heretical doctrines in defiance of Zoroastrian belief
    d. Buddhist teachings

8. Mani may have been the first person
    a. to edit the Zoroastrian sacred books
    b. consciously to "found" a new religious tradition
    c. to create a "scripture" for his followers
    d. both b and c

9. Manichaeism is significant because
    a. its adherents probably carried the Eastern planetary calendar to the West
    b. it established a new justice system for Islam
    c. its ideas figured in both Christian and Islamic heresies
    d. it refused to challenge Christian and Islamic religious theologies

10. The official Persian dialect of the Sassanid empire was
    a. *Shahanshah*
    b. *Pahlavi*
    c. *Kshatriyas*
    d. *Jati*

11. The claim of the Gupta era to being India's golden age of culture could be sustained solely on the basis of
    a. its architecture and sculpture
    c. its wall paintings
    b. the drama and verse of Kalidasa
    d. all of the above

12. In the *Dharmashastra* of Manu, we find
    a. the primary explanation of Hindu theology
    b. the classic statement of the four-class theory of social hierarchy
    c. an engaging work of poetry
    d. a compilation of Gupta dramatic works

13. The caste system
    a. was considered a necessary evil in Gupta society
    b. was only applied to the region of northern India
    c. gave great stability and security to the individual and to society
    d. all of the above

14. Indian reverence for all forms of life is embodied in the principle of
    a. *ahimsa*
    c. *bhakti*
    b. *jati*
    d. *maya*

15. The two main strands of Buddhist religious tradition were the
    a. Mahayana and Theravada
    c. *nirvana* and *maya*
    b. *stupas* and *sutras*
    d. *bodhisattvas* and *tirthas*

16. The Parthians
    a. rejected the Iranian imperial and cultural traditions of the Achaemenids
    b. continued the Iranian imperial and cultural traditions of the Achaemenids
    c. outlawed all religions, except for Zoroastrianism
    d. both a and c

17. Zoroastrian orthodoxy recognized which four main classes?
    a. priests, merchants, warriors, and peasants
    b. noble, merchants, priests, and slaves
    c. priests, warriors, scribes, and peasants
    d. priests, warriors, merchants, and peasants

18. Mazdak preached
    a. pessimism about the evil state of the world
    b. asceticism
    c. vegetarianism
    d. all of the above

19. A major factor that allowed for the formation of a single civilization throughout the Indian subcontinent during the Gupta period was
    a. the economic power of the Guptas
    b. the spread of Christianity
    c. the relative peace and security of the period
    d. innovations in transportation and communication

20. The Gupta empire collapsed
    a. after the invasion of the Huns in the fifth century C.E.
    b. due to religious conflicts
    c. because of corrupt and incompetent rulers
    d. both b and c

21. Most Hindus
       a. worship all deities as equal manifestations of the Ultimate
       b. view one deity as Supreme Lord, but other deities as lesser manifestations of the Ultimate
       c. attach importance to sacred places
       d. both a and b

22. Mahayana means
       a. those devoted to Buddha
       b. Great Vehicle of salvation
       c. Little Vehicle of salvation
       d. both a and b

23. A Bodhisattva is
       a. someone who postpones his own nirvana
       b. a Hindu priest
       c. a Mahayana monk
       d. both a and c

24. Theraveda Buddhism
       a. was based on the scriptural collection of the teaching of Buddha
       b. was based on devotion to bodhisattvas
       c. becam popular in China
       d. is known as the Great Vehicle of salvation

25. With the decline of Rome, Indian culture
       a. could expand to the West
       b. transmitted it culture to the Mediterranean
       c. transmitted its culture to Southeast Asia and China
       d. both a and b

When

1. Chosroes Anosharvan is considered the greatest Sassanid king. How long did he reign? Do you think the length of his reign contributed to his success?

2. Most chronologies in this book focus on rulers. What do the inclusion of priests, monks, and philosophers in the chronologies in this chapter tell you about Iran and India during the period covered in this chapter?

3. Including the revival under Harsha, how long was the Gupta period?

4. What event ended the Persian empire in 651 C.E.?

Where

Using Map 10-1 on page 212 of your textbook, answer the following questions.

1. The three empires on the map were connected by trade. Was this trade conducted over land or by sea?

2. Judging by the locations of major cities and topography (physical features), do you think the Sassanids had closer contact with the Roman-Byzantine empire or the Gupta empire? Why?

3. Why is India called a subcontinent? What topographical (physical) features separate it from the rest of Asia?

How and Why

1.   How did the Sassanid empire develop after the fall of the Parthians? What benefit did the empire receive from the Byzantine state? What were the principal economic bases of the empire?

2.   In what ways can the Gupta period (320-450) truly be considered a "Golden Age"? What was the extent of the boundaries during the time? Why did the empire collapse after 550? What was the importance of the movement of culture south to the Tamil?

3.   What are the main tenets of the Hindu faith? How did the caste system strengthen the major beliefs of the society and what benefits did it offer? How did Hinduism influence Buddhism during this time period?

4.   What were the main tenets of the Buddhist faith in the Gupta period? Why did the Mahayanan traditions become popular in East Asia and China? What was the importance of merit in the Buddhist faith?

5.   What were the major religious issues in the Sassanid empire? What were the tenets of Zoroastrianism and what changes did it undergo?

6.   Why was Manichaeism so attractive and why did the Zoroastrians oppose it? How did Manichaeism influence Christianity and Islam?

Map Labeling

Study Map 10-1 on page 212 of your textbook. Note the interconnection between the Sassanid, Gupta, Roman-Byzantine, and Chinese civilizations. On the map provided on the next page shade in the Gupta, Sassanid, and Roman-Byzantine empires using different colors or shades. Trace the major trade routes.

MULTIPLE CHOICE ANSWER KEY *(with page references)*

1. B (208)	11. D (213)	21. D (215)
2. C (209)	12. B (214)	22. B (217)
3. D (209)	13. C (214)	23. B (217)
4. A (209)	14. A (215)	24. A (217)
5. C (210)	15. A (216)	25. C (213)
6. D (210)	16. B (208)	
7. A (210)	17. C (209)	
8. D (210)	18. D (211)	
9. C (210)	19. C (211)	
10. B (211)	20. A (212)	

Chapter Eleven
The Formation of Islamic Civilization (622-945)

Practice Test

1. The basic ideas and ideals of the Islamic worldview derived from a single, prophetic-revelatory event:
   a. the submission of Muslims to the will of *Allah*
   b. Muhammad's proclamation of the Qur'an
   c. the Muslim victory over Charles Martel at the battle of Tours
   d. none of the above

2. The town of Mecca was important because
   a. of its famous sanctuary, the Ka'ba
   b. it was a center of the caravan trade
   c. of its strategic geopolitical location in the center of Arabia
   d. both a and b

3. The notion that Islam was a "religion of the desert"
   a. is largely untrue
   b. enabled it to spread among the desert tribes
   c. allowed it to be carried along the caravan routes
   d. both b and c

4. Muhammad was motivated to establish a new religious tradition because
   a. he was troubled by the frivolous disregard for morality among Arabs
   b. his poverty was so intense that he had no hope
   c. of the intense political control of the priesthoods by tribal leaders
   d. all of the above

5. The message of the Qur'an was that
   a. the way to paradise lay in proper gratitude to God for forgiveness and guidance
   b. idolatrous worship of false gods would not be tolerated
   c. immorality and injustice to the weak and less fortunate was wrong
   d. all of the above

6. The Hegira refers to
   a. the early Islamic conquest of Egypt
   b. a pilgrimage to Mecca
   c. Muhammad's "emigration" to Medina
   d. the Muslim lunar year

7. Jews, Christians, and other "people of Scripture" who accepted Islamic political authority were
   a. ignored by the Muslim community
   b. tolerated by Islam, but assessed a head tax
   c. excluded from business dealings by Islam, but were not persecuted
   d. considered "unclean" and exiled from Muslim communities

8. Muhammad's successor, Abu Bakr,
   a. lost control of the *Umma* and forced a split between Meccan and Medinan factions
   b. conquered the Byzantine and Sassanid territories of the Fertile Crescent
   c. reestablished nominal religious conformity over the whole of Arabia
   d. both a and b

9. Arab Islamic armies
   a. conquered the lands from Egypt to Iran and united them under one rule
   b. controlled parts of southern France after successfully defeating Charles Martel
   c. never penetrated the Indus region of Sind
   d. both b and c

10. What gave Islamic conquests overall permanence was the
   a. vitality of the new faith
   b. fact that there was relatively little bloodshed or destruction of property
   c. appointment of capable governors and astute administrative policies
   d. all of the above

11. The Shi'ites
   a. espoused a total egalitarianism among the faithful
   b. believed that the leadership of the *Umma* belonged to the best Muslim
   c. were called "seceders" who broke away from the leadership of Ali
   d. none of the above

12. The height of caliphal power and splendor came
   a. during the Umayyad rule about 650 C.E.
   b. after the Umayyad decline under the Abbasids about 750 C.E.
   c. under the rule of Ali and the Kharijites about 600 C.E.
   d. under the Seljuk emirs about 1055

13. In the mid-eighth century paper manufacture was introduced to the Islamic world from
   a. Europe   c. China
   b. India   d. Egypt

14. Islamic culture took over the tradition of rational inquiry from the Hellenistic world as demonstrated by the
   a. preservation and translation of Greek scientific and philosophical works
   b. dominant Greek influence in Islamic architecture
   c. insistence that *imams* learn Greek as a part of their formal schooling
   d. both a and b

15. The *Hadith* was a
   a. significant genre of Arabic writing
   b. compilation of Islamic poetry based on the Arabic ode
   c. collection of the words and deeds ascribed to Muhammad that formed the basic unit of history and biography
   d. book of stories about the pomp and splendor of the Abbasid court

16. The Qur'an states that
   a. Muhammad is God's only prophet
   b. Muhammad is one in a long line of prophets
   c. Muhammad was given the final iteration of God's message
   d. both a and c

17. The pilgrimage to Mecca is known as the
   a. Hegira
   b. Hajj
   c. Umma
   d. Ka'ba

18. Which of the following factors accounts for the success of early Muslim conquests?
    a. the weakened military and economic conditions of the Byzantines and Sassanids
    b. forced conversions of Christians and Jews
    c. brilliant Arab generals
    d. the voluntary conversion of the Sassanids

19. Which of the following is a title for a leader in the Muslim world?
    a. caliph
    b. imam
    c. amir
    d. all of the above

20. The ulama are
    a. the original companions of Muhammad
    b. court advisors to the caliphs
    c. scholars who preserved, interpreted, and applied the Qur'an
    d. both a and c

21. Acceptance into the Umma was conditioned upon
    a. a thorough knowledge of the Qur'an
    b. submission to God and Muslim precepts
    c. adoption of Arab culture and customs
    d. attachment ot an Arab patron

22. Kharijites believed that
    a. the leader of the Umma should be the best Muslim
    b. the leader of the Umma should be a descendent of Muhammad through Ali
    c. Qur'anic principles should be modified to accommodate non-Arab converts
    d. both a and c

23. According to the centrist, or Sunni, position, authority in the Umma resides in
    a. the direct descendents of Muhammad through Ali
    b. the Qur'an alone
    c. the Qur'an, the precedent of Muhammad, and the consensus of Muslims
    d. the interpretive efforts and consensus of Muslims

24. Full conversion of the populace of the Islamic empire
    a. preceded the centralization of power and development of Islamic institutions
    b. lagged behind centralization of power and development of Islamic institutions
    c. occurred simultaneously with the centralization of power and development of Islamic institutions
    d. occurred immediately upon conquest

25. In 945 the Shi'ite Buyid clan
    a. restored the Abbasid dynasty
    b. supported the Spanish Umayyad dynsty against the Abbasids
    c. reduced the Abbasids to puppets
    d. were crushed by the Abbasids

When

1. How long did it take Arab armies to expand to Spain in the West and the Indus in the East, after the death of Muhammad?

2. How long after the death of Muhammad was the first Arab civil war over succession?

3. Measuring from the Caliphate of Umar to the rise of the Buyid amirs, how long was the Caliphate an important institution in the Arab-Muslim empire?

4. When did the first Shi'ite dynasty form?

5. During which century was Arab culture most heavily influenced by Greek, Persian, and Indian literary and scientific culture?

Where

Study Map 11-1 on page 227 of your textbook. Note the different stages of conquest and the territory gained in each period. How quickly did the Islamic empire expand when compared to other empires that you have studied such as Alexander's (p. 69), the Roman (p. 106), the Han (p. 143), the Mongol (p. 179), and the T'ang (p. 159)?

How and Why

1.   Discuss the importance of Mecca to the development of Arab unity. What role did Medina play? Was Islam a "religion of the desert"?

2.   What were the main reasons for the success of the Arab conquests? What geographic areas were conquered by 732? Why did the older empires fail to stop these invasions?

3.   What are the main concepts of the doctrine of Islam? How is this faith different from Christianity? What is the position of women in the faith? What is the importance of other faiths to this movement?

4.   What was the importance of the *umma* to Muslim society? How were religious minorities and non-Arab converts treated? How did the change of the Islamic capital to Baghdad affect the empire?

5.   What was the impact of the Shi'ite movement on the Islamic faith? Why did it fail to dominate the majority of believers in the faith? What are the main differences between the Shi'ites and the Sunnis?

6.   Describe the main reasons for the decline of the Arab empire. What was the role of the Mamluks in the process of decline? How important was local control in the decline of empire? What were lasting contributions of the Arab empire?

Map Labeling

By 750, Muslims had come to dominate most areas south and east of the Mediterranean Sea. Identify these locations and place them on the map provided.

1. Persia
2. Arabia
3. Palestine
4. Egypt
5. Algeria
6. Spain
7. Cordoba
8. Mecca
9. Medina
10. Jerusalem
11. Damascus
12. Baghdad

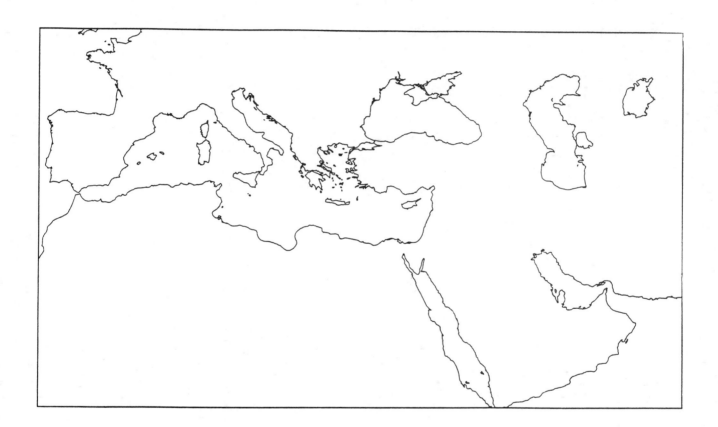

MULTIPLE CHOICE ANSWER KEY *(with page references)*

1. B (222)	11. D (231)	21. B (230)
2. D (222)	12. B (232)	22. A (231)
3. A (222)	13. C (233)	23. C (232)
4. A (223)	14. A (235)	24. B (233)
5. D (223)	15. C (235)	25. C (234)
6. C (225)	16. D (224)	
7. B (226)	17. B (225)	
8. C (226)	18. A (226)	
9. A (226)	19. D (228)	
10. D (227)	20. C (230)	

Chapter Twelve
The Early Middle Ages in the West to 1000:
The Birth of Europe

Practice Test

1. Scutage was
    a. a small villa
    b. a monetary payment by a vassal to avoid military service
    c. the obligation of a monk toward the monastic rule
    d. the obligation of the Holy Roman Emperor to protect the papacy

2. During the early Middle Ages, manorialism and feudalism were
    a. destroyed by the barbarian invaders
    b. unsuccessful in ordering society
    c. successful for coping with unprecedented chaos on local levels
    d. successful in establishing trade on a regional level in Europe

3. Justinian's *Corpus Juris Civilis*
    a. centralized leadership of the eastern Roman Empire
    b. had little immediate impact on medieval common law
    c. provided freedom of worship for Arian Christians
    d. established the primacy of the Patriarch of Constantinople

4. As a result of the Germanic invasions of the fourth century, Western Europe
    a. was transformed into a savage land
    b. retained its cultural strength, if not its military control
    c. lost its Roman culture, which was replaced by new Germanic institutions
    d. both a and c

5. Arianism had been condemned in 325 at the Council of
    a. Nicaea   c. Ferrara-Florence
    b. Chalcedon   d. Constantinople

6. In terms of territory, political power, and culture, which of the following periods in Byzantine history was the greatest:
    a. 324-632   c. 632-1071
    b. 1071-1250   d. 1250-1453

7. The imperial goal of the Byzantine emperor in the East was to
    a. centralize government
    b. impose legal and doctrinal conformity
    c. institute a policy reflected in the phrase, "one God, one empire, one religion"
    d. all of the above

8. In 732 the Franks
    a. swore fealty to the Byzantine emperor
    b. were defeated by Muslim Arabs at Tours
    c. defeated a Muslim Arab army at Tours
    d. defeated a Seljuk Turk army at Tours

9. The Arab invasions and presence in the Mediterranean area during the early Middle Ages
    a. cut off all trade with East Asia
    b. created the essential conditions for the birth of Western Europe as a distinctive cultural entity
    c. contributed to the imposition of Eastern trade and cultural influence on the West
    d. provided a protective barrier between Western Europe and hostile Persia

10. Monastic culture
    a. declined with the barbarian invasions   c. contributed to the division of Christendom
    b. strengthened the church during the Middle Ages   d. resisted papal primacy

11. The doctrine of "papal primacy"
    a. raised the Roman pontiff to an unassailable supremacy within the church
    b. confirmed the supremacy of bishops within their urban jurisdiction
    c. established papal legitimacy in defining church doctrine
    d. both a and c

12. The major factor in the religious break between East and West revolved around the
    a. question of doctrinal authority and papal primacy
    b. *filioque* clause of the Nicene-Constantinopolitan Creed
    c. iconoclastic controversy of the early eighth century
    d. all of the above

13. The founder of the first Frankish dynasty was
    a. Charlemagne   c. Clovis
    b. Pepin the Short   d. Charles Martel

14. The head of Charlemagne's palace school was
    a. Einhard   c. Martin of Tours
    b. Alcuin of York   d. Lothar the Wise

15. Under feudalism, the lord's obligations to his vassals included
    a. an obligation to protect them from physical harm
    b. investment of the vassal with a portion of church land
    c. supplying them with his armor and fighting equipment
    d. none of the above

16. In 1071 the Byzantine Empire suffered a major defeat at the hands of
    a. Arabs
    b. Franks
    c. Turks
    d. Huns

17. Throughout the early Middle Ages, the Byzantine Empire
    a. was a constant threat to western Europe
    b. protected western Europe from Asian armies
    c. was a conduit of classical learning to the West
    d. both a and b

18. The two major forms of monasticism in the early Middle Ages were
    a. hermit monasticism and individual monasticism
    b. hermit monasticism and communal monasticism
    c. mystical monasticism and communal monasticism
    d. hermit monasticism and mystical monasticism

19. Before becoming kings of the Franks, the Carolingians served as
    a. counts
    b. directors of the palace schools
    c. mayors of the palace
    d. popes

20. In the Frankish Church, bishops
   a. became lords, appointed by the king
   b. remained aloof from royal politics and government
   c. were employed as royal agents
   d. both a and c

21. Which of the following was not a title that Charlemagne assumed?
   a. King of the Greeks
   b. King of the Franks
   c. King of the Lombards
   d. Emperor of the Romans

22. After Charlemagne's imperial coronation
   a. the eastern emperors launched an invasion of Western Europe
   b. the eastern emperors recognized his title
   c. Charlemagne invaded the Byzantine Empire
   d. both a and c

23. The part of the land known as the demesne
   a. was rented out to peasants
   b. was reserved for hunting by the lords
   c. was farmed by peasants for the lord
   d. lay fallow

24. Someone who surrenders his property to a lord in exchange for protection is called a
   a. freeman
   b. serf
   c. slave
   d. Magyar

25. To maintain growing armies, landed nobles gave their vassals
   a. the right to collect taxes
   b. an annual salary
   c. a benefice
   d. a demesne

When

1. Which groups invaded Europe in the fifth century? The eighth? The tenth?

2. Which events between 732 and 800 lead to the rise of the Carolingian dynasty?

3. Which events between 843 and 950 caused the eventual fall of the Carolingian dynasty?

4. When did the Ottonian dynasty replace the Carolingian dynasty in Germany?

5. When did the Capetian dynasty replace the Carolingian dynasty in France?

81

Where

1. Study Map 12-1 on page 242 of your textbook. How many Germanic tribes invaded the Roman Empire? Which tribes penetrated the empire the farthest and had the greatest impact on Roman civilization? Why in particular did the Goths enter the empire? Compare this map with Map 12-5 on page 255. From what directions was Europe invaded in the tenth and eleventh centuries?

2. Using Map 12-3 on page 249 of your textbook, fill in the blanks with the appropriate letter.

A. part of Charlemagne's kingdom by 814   B. tributary kingdom   C. Byzantine

Aquitaine   _____

Duchy of Benevento   _____

Bohemia   _____

Saxons   _____

Burgundy   _____

Moravia   _____

How and Why

1.   Historians have often disagreed as to when the ancient world ended and the Middle Ages began. Do you think the end of the ancient world is characterized by the collapse of Roman power in the West, the triumph of Christianity, or the rise of Islam?

2.   Why were the barbarian tribes successful in defeating the Romans militarily? In what ways did the Roman Empire retain its cultural strength? Did the Germanic tribes become more Romanized than Rome became Germanized?

3.   Trace the growth of the Frankish kingdom, including its relations with the church, down to Charlemagne. Then, describe Charlemagne, the man and the ruler, and his society. How and why did his empire break up?

4.   Trace the history of Christianity down to the coronation of Charlemagne in 800. What distinctive features characterized the early church? What role did the church play in the world after the fall of the western empire?

5.   How and why was the history of the eastern half of the Roman Empire so different from the western half? What factors contributed to the growth of a distinctive Western European culture?

6.   How and why did feudal society get started? What were the essential ingredients of feudalism and how easily do you think it would be for our modern society to "slip back" into a feudal society?

Map Labeling

Study map 12-2 on page 245 of your textbook. Using the blank map, shade in the Byzantine Empire in 527, use dotted lines to show the extent of the Byzantine Empire after the conquests of Justinian, and use solid lines to show the boundaries of the kingdoms of the Franks and Visigoths. Identify and label the following cities: Constantinople, Ravenna, Toledo, Rome, and Jerusalem.

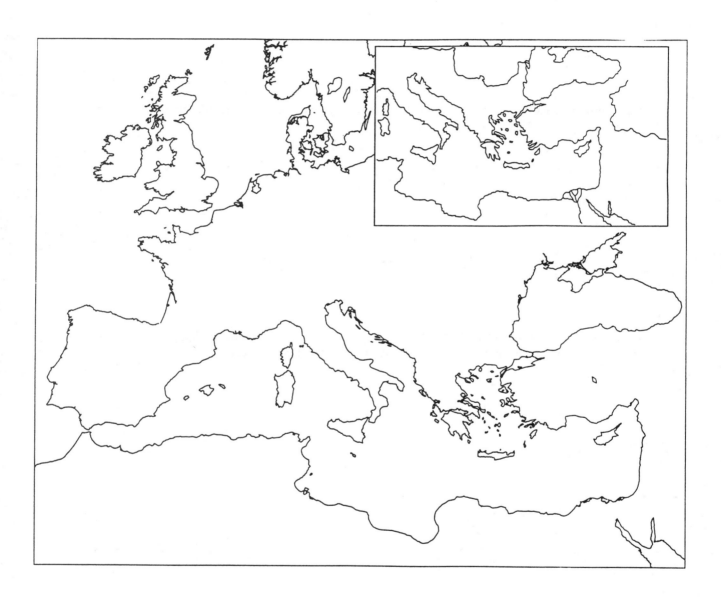

MULTIPLE CHOICE ANSWER KEY *(with page references)*

1. B (255)

2. C (240)

3. B (241)

4. B (240)

5. A (240)

6. A (240)

7. D (241)

8. C (244)

9. B (244)

10. B (246)

11. D (246)

12. D (246)

13. C (247)

14. B (250)

15. A (255)

16. C (242)

17. D (242)

18. B (245)

19. C (247)

20. D (248)

21. A (248)

22. B (249)

23. C (251)

24. B (252)

25. C (254)

Chapter Thirteen
The Islamic Heartlands and India
(ca. 1000-1500)

Practice Test

1. By the mid-tenth century in the Islamic world,
   a. centralized caliphal power had broken down
   b. regional Islamic states with distinctive political and cultural configurations now dominated
   c. the stability of the Islamic *ulama* had been maintained
   d. both a and b

2. During the period 1000-1500, what two Asian steppe peoples rose to dominance?
   a. Visigoths and Turks
   b. Fatimids and Umayyads
   c. Mongols and Turks
   d. Ghaznavids and Saljuqs

3. From the elevnth century onward, the *ulama's* power and fixity as a class were expressed in the institution of the
   a. *madrasa*
   b. *fiqh*
   c. *Hadith*
   d. none of the above

4. In the Islamic world, theological positions were most often determined by
   a. sectarian identity
   b. orthodoxy (belief)
   c. orthopraxy (practice)
   d. both a and b

5. Sufi piety stresses
   a. Islamic law and an observance of Muslim duties
   b. the spiritual and mystical dimensions of Islam
   c. Gnostic and Neo-Platonic philosophy as a foundation of belief
   d. none of the above

6. The two Shi'ite groups that emerged as the most influential were the
   a. *imams* and Batinis
   b. Seveners and Twelvers
   c. Qarmatians and Fatimids
   d. Sunnis and Seveners

7. The western half of the Islamic world after the tenth century developed a regional focus in
   a. Spain and Moroccan North Africa
   b. Egypt and Syria
   c. Palestine and Anatolia
   d. all of the above

8. Abd al-Rahman I was important because he
   a. founded the cosmopolitan tradition of Umayyad Spanish culture at Cordoba
   b. upset the stability of Islamic Spain by accentuating the rift between religious factions
   c. closed the mosque-university of Cordoba
   d. both b and c

9. The *Reconquista*, or Reconquest, refers to the
   a. victory of the Almoravids over the Almohads
   b. victory of Abd al-Rahman I over the Almoravids
   c. victory of Spanish Christian rulers led by El Cid over the Muslims
   d. collapse of Fatimid power throughout the Mediterranean

10. The Almoravids originated as a
    a. religious-warrior brotherhood among Berber nomads
    b. splinter group of the Isma'ili assassins
    c. Sunni religious brotherhood
    d. Sufi religious brotherhood

11. The heirs of the Fatimids and Saladin in the eastern Mediterranean were the
    a. Kipchak Turks   c. Berbers
    b. Mamluks   d. Saljuqs

12. In the mid-thirteenth century, the Mongols were led on the path of conquest in the Islamic world by
    a. Genghis Khan   c. Hulagu Khan
    b. Ghazi warriors   d. Tammerlane

13. Islamic civilization in India was formed by the
    a. Mamluks who invaded Indian lands and imposed Islam on the population
    b. Sufi order which acted as missionaries
    c. creative interaction of invading foreigners with indigenous peoples
    d. both b and c

14. The chief obstacle to Islamic expansion in India was the
    a. military prowess and tradition of a Hindu warrior class
    b. topographical defense afforded by so many rivers and a difficult climate
    c. influence of the great trading city of Kashmir
    d. presence of Mongol armies in the western regions of India

15. Hindu religion and culture
    a. was eliminated in areas of Muslim control
    b. continued to flourish even in areas of Muslim control
    c. broke down with the decline of the *bhakti*
    d. both a and c

16. The major Islamic presence in the Mediterranean from the tenth to the twelfth century was that of the
    a. Mamluks
    b. Almohads
    c. Fatimids
    d. Almoravids

17. The Mamluks enjoyed prosperity after 1300
    a. due to the weakness of the Byzantines
    b. as trade relations improved with Mongol domains
    c. because of a strong allegiance to Shi'ite Islam
    d. both a and c

18. The Saljuks
    a. were the first major Turkish dynasty of Islam
    b. ruled as caliphs in Baghdad
    c. extended Muslim rule at Byzantine expense
    d. both a and c

19. Hulagu ruled Iran
    a. as the viceroy of the Great Khan
    b. as a Muslim convert
    c. from Baghdad
    d. both a and c

20. Hindus from the lower classes
        a. were often converted by Shi'ite missionaries
        b. were the most resistant to Muslim missionary activities
        c. were often converted by Sufi missionaries
        d. incorporated Allah into the Hindu pantheon of gods

21. Indian Muslims
        a. were always susceptible to Hindu influence
        b. were absorbed into Hindu culture
        c. were never completely absorbed into Hindu culture
        d. both a and c

22. Which Indian language developed in response to the increasing need of Hindus and Muslims to communicate?
        a. Tamil
        b. Urdu-Hindi
        c. Persian
        d. Sanskrit

23. The most important independent Islamic state was
        a. the Bahmanids
        b. the Sayyids
        c. the Rajputs
        d. the Ilkhans

24. Timur-I Lang
        a. conquered much of the Middle East and Central Asia
        b. created chaos across the entire Islamic world
        c. led the last great steppe invasion
        d. all of the above

25. The Ghaznavids are notable for
        a. their revival of Indian culture
        b. their persecution of Shi'ites
        c. their patronage of Persian culture
        d. their patronage of Arabic culture

When

1. Which events in the early 1260s halted the Mongol advance into Muslim territories?

2. What is the chronological relationship between the Crusade in western Islamic lands and Turkish and Mongol invasions of eastern Islamic lands?

3. When did non-Arab rulers begin to dominate western Islamic lands?

4. When did non-Arab rulers begin to dominate eastern Islamic lands?

5. Which dynasty ruled longest as sultans of Delhi?

Where

Study the major ruling dynasties that are noted on Map 13-1 on page 260 of your textbook. It is important to connect the political and cultural activities of these dynasties with their geographical locations. What are "Khanates" and which empire controlled them? How did Ottomans differ from Saljuqs and Mamluks?

How and Why

1.   Describe the political, social, and economic conditions in the Islamic heartlands from 945 to 1500. What was the role of the Sunni and Shi'ite sects in this time period? How did the Mongols and the Turks alter the culture in the heartland? Why did Islam survive these outside invasions?

2.   Discuss the cultural developments in Spain from 945-1500. Why was Cordoba considered an example of cultural progress? Why were certain Christian and Jewish groups persecuted in this time of great cultural development?

3. What was the impact of Tamerlane on the Islamic heartland? Why did the Mongols fail to stop this invasion? What motivated the conquests of Tamerlane?

4. The period from roughly 1000 to 1500 saw the spread of Islam as a lasting religious, cultural, and political force in world history. Where specifically did Islam spread and how was it introduced to these new regions? Why was it successful?

5. From the beginning, Muslim leaders faced the problem of ruling an India dominated by an utterly different culture and religion. Discuss the problems of Muslim conquerors. What were their primary obstacles to stable rule and how did they deal with them?

6. During the Muslim infiltration of India from 1000 to 1500, what happened to the other religious traditions that Islam encountered? Most specifically, address the fate of the Jain tradition, Buddhism, and Hinduism.

Map Labeling

By 1500, Islamic sovereignty had spread widely. Study Map 13-2 on page 269 of your textbook. On the map provided, shade-in the area where there was either Islamic political control or a majority Muslim population.

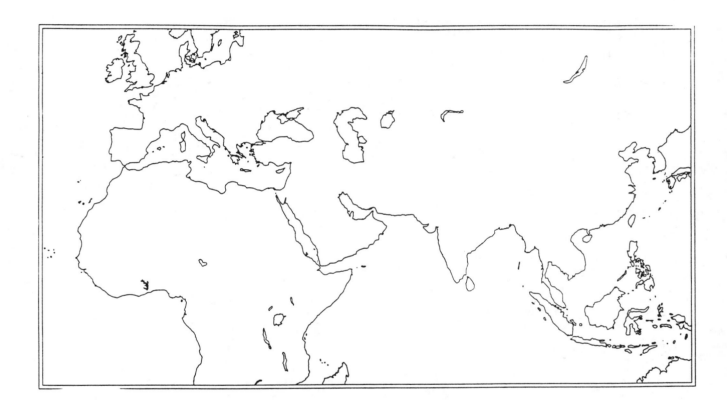

MULTIPLE CHOICE ANSWER KEY *(with page references)*

1. D (260)	11. B (265)	21. D (271)
2. C (260)	12. C (267)	22. B (271)
3. A (261)	13. C (268)	23. A (269)
4. C (261)	14. A (269)	24. D (268)
5. B (261)	15. B (271)	25. C (266)
6. B (262)	16. C (265)	
7. D (264)	17. B (265)	
8. A (264)	18. D (267)	
9. C (264)	19. A (268)	
10. A (264)	20. C (270)	

Practice Test

1. Difficulties confront scholars trying to understand the ancient civilizations of the Americas because
   a. Andean civilizations never developed writing
   b. Mesoamerican civilizations never developed writing
   c. Andean writing displays a pro-Spanish bias
   d. most of the evidence is from an oral tradition

2. Mesoamerica extends from
   a. central Mexico into Central America
   b. Central America to Brazil
   c. North America to Mexico
   d. Chile north to Panama

3. The "classic" or high point of Mesoamerican civilization occurred during which period?
   a. 2000 B.C.E. - 150 C.E.   c. 150 - 900 C.E.
   b. 900 - 1521 C.E.   d. 800 - 2000 B.C.E.

4. The people of the Americas never developed the wheel because they
   a. were inferior engineers   c. had no ready access to wood and iron
   b. had no large draft animals   d. were nomadic hunter-gatherers

5. The most conspicuous feature of Olmec La Venta was
   a. massive stone heads   c. the Great pyramid
   b. clay pottery   d. obsidian statues

6. The monumental architecture at San Lorenzo suggests that Olmec society
   a. was dominated by an elite class of ruler-priests
   b. maintained social equality between the sexes
   c. was monotheistic
   d. both a and c

7. The Mesoamerican calendar is based on
   a. a lunar year of 260 days
   b. two interlocking solar cycles
   c. a century of 35 years
   d. both b and c

8. The Pyramid of the Sun is closely associated with which civilization?
   a. Teotihuacan   c. Guatemala
   b. Inca   d. Maya

9. Maya civilization differed from other Mesoamerican civilizations because they
   a. had a system of writing
   b. left records on imperishable materials
   c. used books
   d. both a and b

10. The Toltec civilization
    a. lasted for over a thousand years
    b. influenced the Aztecs in terms of religion and mythology
    c. held a powerful empire that included the Maya centers
    d. all of the above

11. After a conquest, the Aztecs
    a. destroyed their enemy's cities
    b. did not demand tribute in goods or labor
    c. left the local elite in power and ruled indirectly
    d. both b and c

12. Central to Aztec ideology was
    a. the death of the river god
    b. the resurrection of four sun goddesses
    c. human sacrifice
    d. flowers that signified the birth of civilization

13. Which of the following is the correct chronological order for Andean civilizations?
    a. Chavín de Huantar, Moche, Chimu, Inca
    b. Moche, Chimu, Inca, Chavín de Huantar
    c. Chimu, Moche, Chavín de Huantar, Inca
    d. Chavín de Huantar, Chimu, Moche, Inca

14. When Francisco Pizarro arrived in 1532, the Incan Empire was
    a. in decline
    b. one of the largest states in the world
    c. confined to the center of Machu Picchu
    d. not yet free from the control of the Chanca people

15. The Incas ruled their empire by
    a. extracting tribute from their subject peoples
    b. relying on various forms of labor taxation
    c. employing people in full-time state service
    d. both b and c

16. Mayan religion
    a. was practiced only by the priesthood
    b. deeply informed the social and political realms
    c. was sharply separated from politics
    d. both a and c.

17. Among the important Mayan religious rituals were
    a. bloodletting ceremonies
    b. ballgames
    c. sacrifice of captives
    d. all of the above

18. The collapse of Classical Period civilization in the southern lowlands
    a. has not been explained by historians
    b. was caused by climactic change
    c. was caused by invasion
    d. was caused by inept rulers

19. Aztec society was
    a. egalitarian, democratic, and pacifistic
    b. hierarchical, authoritarian, and pacifistic
    c. hierarchical, authoritarian, and militaristic
    d. egalitarian, democratic, and militaristic

20. Above all, Aztec society was organized for
    a. religion
    b. war
    c. peace
    d. both a and c

21. Women in Aztec society
    a. could own and inherit property
    b. were not allowed in public
    c. were excluded from high authority
    d. both a and c

22. The Nazca were renowned for
    a. war
    b. large urban centers
    c. textiles and fine pottery
    d. both a and b

23. In about 1470 the Chimu empire
    a. was swept away by the Inca Empire
    b. was swept away by the Huari
    c. united with the Incas to dominate the Andean region
    d. was conquered by the Spanish

24. The Inca enlarged their empire through
    a. alliance
    b. intimidation
    c. conquest
    d. all of the above

25. The rise of the Huari is associated with
    a. massive obsidian stautes
    b. techniques for terracing and irrigation
    c. the production of textiles and fine pottery
    d. both a and c

When

1. When does Post-Classical Mesoamerican civilization end? When does Late Horizon Andean civilization end? What accounts for the similarity?

2. Did civilization arise earlier in Mesoamerica or the Andean region?

Where

1. Using the scales on Map 14-1 on page 278 of your textbook, estimate the size of the Aztec and Inca Empires.

2. Referring to Map 14-2 on page 285 of your textbook, list the modern nations that now exist in what was Mesoamerica. In what modern country do most Mesoamerican sites exist?

How and Why

1. What are some of the difficulties that have confronted scholars trying to understand the ancient civilizations of the Americas? What is the nature of the evidence?

2. Discuss the Olmec centers of San Lorenzo and La Venta. What have archaeologists found there that tell us about the Olmec civilization? Refer specifically to the art, architecture, and public services.

3. Discuss the importance of the Maya culture and its influence in southern Mesoamerica. What was life like in such Maya centers as Tikal? What were the greatest contributions of the Maya?

4.   The text notes that the Aztecs had an "extractive empire." What does this mean? How did the organization of the Aztec empire and the treatment of subject peoples differ from that of the Incas?

5.   The practice of human sacrifice is of particular importance in Mesoamerican civilizations. What was the religious significance behind it and how was it practiced, particularly by the Aztecs? Was human sacrifice a moral evil? What did the Spanish think? Could the Spanish justify their obliteration of the Aztec civilization in an ethical sense?

6.   Discuss the Andean civilizations of Tiwanaku, Huari, and Chimu. How were these empires administered? What was the system known as the mita?

Map Labeling

Study Map 14-2 on page 285 of your textbook.   On the map provided for you, shade in the Aztec and Inca Empires. Identify and label the major urban centers of each empire. Circle the capitals of each empire.

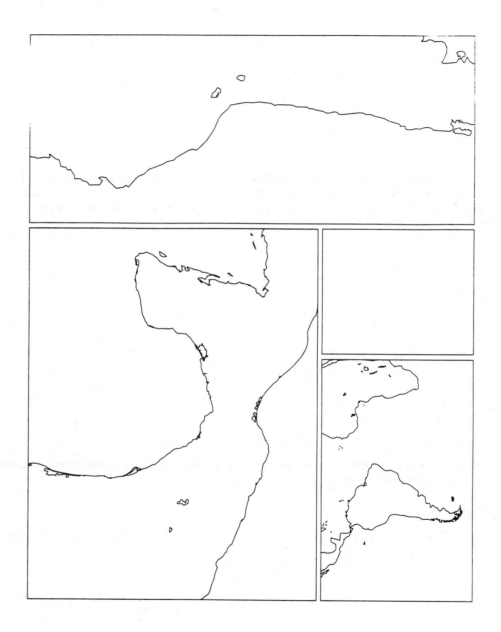

MULTIPLE CHOICE ANSWER KEY *(with page references)*

1. A (276)	11. C (284)	21. D (288)
2. A (276)	12. C (285)	22. C (289)
3. C (277)	13. A (289)	23. A (291)
4. B (277)	14. B (291)	24. D (292)
5. C (278)	15. D (292)	25. B (290)
6. A (278)	16. B (282)	
7. B (279)	17. D (282)	
8. A (280)	18. A (283)	
9. B (281)	19. C (287)	
10. B (284)	20. B (288)	

Chapter Fifteen
Europe to the Early 1500s:
Revival, Decline, and Renaissance

Practice test

1. The High Middle Ages (1000-1300)
   a. mark a period of intellectual flowering and synthesis
   b. saw the borders of Western Europe largely secured against foreign invaders
   c. saw a revolution in agriculture that increased both food supplies and population
   d. all of the above

2. Which of the following was a reform instituted by Pope Gregory VII?
   a. the condemnation of abbots who held political office
   b. the prevention of lay investiture of clergy
   c. the rejection of excommunication as a weapon of the church
   d. both a and b

3. The Concordat of Worms in 1122 required that
   a. the emperor formally renounce his power to invest bishops with the ring and staff of office
   b. the emperor give up the right to nominate or veto a candidate for bishop
   c. the pope invest bishops with fiefs
   d. none of the above

4. The early Crusades were
   a. undertaken for patently mercenary as well as religious motives
   b. successful in controlling the Holy Land politically and militarily
   c. to a very high degree inspired by genuine religious piety
   d. undertaken to destroy the Byzantine power in the region

5. One of the most important developments in medieval civilization between 1100 and 1300 was
   a. the victory of the Crusaders over the Infidel
   b. the dominance of vassals over their former lords
   c. the lasting victory of church over state
   d. revival of trade and growth of towns

6. The university of Bologna was distinguished as the
   a. main training center for government bureaucrats
   b. center for the revival of Roman law
   c. center for church-sanctioned spiritual studies
   d. originator of the college system

7. The underlying cause for the Hundred Years' War between France and England was the
   a. fact that the French king was a vassal of the English king
   b. French support of the Burgundians
   c. decades of prejudice and animosity between the French and English people
   d. all of the above

8. The lord of a manor had the right to subject his tenets to exactions known as
   a. *corvees*   c. *fides*
   b. *banalities*   d. *coloni*

9. Joan of Arc gave the French people and armies
    a. an alliance with Flanders
    b. the support of the church and papal financial contributions
    c. a legitimate heir to the throne of France
    d. a sense of national identity

10. Although the Hundred Years' War devastated France, it
    a. resulted in the transfer of English culture throughout France
    b. hastened the transition in France to a feudal monarchy
    c. awakened the giant of French nationalism
    d. resulted in lasting trade contacts with England

11. The Black Death
    a. was preceded by years of famine that weakened the populace
    b. followed the trade routes into Europe from England
    c. devastated primarily the rural population of Europe
    d. was preceded by a gradual decline in population

12. Among the social and economic consequences of the plague were a
    a. shrunken labor supply
    b. rise in agricultural prices
    c. decline in the price of luxury and manufactured goods
    d. all of the above

13. After the humiliation of Pope Boniface VIII at the hands of agents of Philip IV,
    a. the Holy Roman Empire was dissolved
    b. the popes retreated to Avignon for sanctuary
    c. vassals of the English king invaded France in support of the pope
    d. never again did popes so seriously threaten kings and emperors

14. Which of the following is in the correct chronological order?
    a. Avignon papacy, Conciliar Movement, Great Schism
    b. Avignon papacy, Great Schism, Conciliar Movement
    c. Great Schism, Avignon papacy, Conciliar Movement
    d. Conciliar Movement, Great Schism, Avignon papacy

15. Humanists were
    a. advocates of a liberal arts program of study
    b. rich merchants who either wrote poetry or painted
    c. supporters of the church
    d. scholars who looked to the present rather than the past for inspiration

16. The Cluny reformers
    a. rejected the subservience of the clergy to papal authority
    b. advocated clerical marriage
    c. rejected the subservience of the clergy to royal authority
    d. were ignored by the papacy

17. Both the Crusades and the Cluny Reform Movement
    a. show the lack of authority of the Pope over European Christians
    b. were outlets for the heightened religious zeal of the twelfth century
    c. reveal that religious zeal in the twelfth century was limited to the clergy
    d. both a and c

18. The growth of towns
 a. improved the lot of serfs
 b. worsened the lot of the serfs
 c. allowed lords to replace serfs with slaves
 d. did not affect rural serfs

19. Guilds
 a. allowed the urban elite to keep artisans and craftspeople out of government
 b. gave artisans and craftspeople a voice in urban government
 c. were aristocratic town councils
 d. both a and c

20. The method of study in medieval universities was called
 a. Humanism
 b. regula
 c. Scholasticism
 d. secular

21. The most important distinction among clergy in the High Middle Ages was between
 a. regular and secular
 b. married and celibate
 c. scholastics and humanists
 d. noble and common

22. Medieval women
 a. were barred from all trades
 b. were prominent in many trades
 c. were considered inferior by the male Christian clergy
 d. both a and b

23. The battle of Bouvines in 1214
 a. resulted in the Norman conquest of England
 b. was a major set back for the Capetian dynasty
 c. unified France around the monarchy
 d. unified England around the monarchy

24. After 1450 unified national monarchies
 a. were left in a shambles by the Black Plague and incessant warfare
 b. progressively replaced feudal government
 c. eliminated the dynastic and chivalric ideals of feudalism
 d. both b and c

25. A cornerstone of French nation building in the fifteenth century was
 a. the collapse of English holdings in France after the Hundred Years' War
 b. the defeat of Charles the Bold and the Duchy of Burgundy
 c. the defeat of Germany at the battle of Bouvines
 d. both a and b

When

1. When did Pope Gregory VII pardon Emperor Henry IV? When did Pope Urban II call the First Crusade? What do these events tell us about the role and power of the papacy at that time?

2. How long did the Crusaders hold Jerusalem?

3. Which event ended the Treaty of Lodi?

4. When were the three invasion of Italy by France?

Where

After studying Map 15-3 on page 399 of your textbook, determine the origin of the Black Death and its introduction to Europe. How fast did the disease travel? Where was it most virulent? In particular, compare the spread of the plague on this map with Map 15-1 on page 308 of your textbook. What similarities can you see, especially in Spain and France? What does this tell you about how the disease spread?

How and Why

1.   What were the main reasons behind the Cluny Reform Movement? What were some of the reforms? How do you account for the success of the movement and what were some of its results?

2.   What major development in western and eastern Europe encouraged the emergence of the crusading movement? What were the political, religious, and economic results of the Crusades? Which do you consider most important and why?

3.   What led to the revival of trade and the growth of towns in the twelfth century? What political and social conditions were essential for a revival of trade? How did towns change medieval society?

4.   Consider the Black Death. What were its causes and why did it spread so quickly throughout western Europe? Where was it most virulent? What were the results of the Black Death and how important do you think disease is in changing the course of history?

5.   What was the Great Schism? How did the church become divided and how was it reunited? Why was the Conciliar Movement a set-back for the papacy?

6.   How would you define "Renaissance Humanism"? In what ways was the Renaissance a break with the Middle Ages and in what ways did it owe its existence to medieval civilization?

Map Labeling

Medieval Germany and Italy were divided lands where disunity and feuding reigned for two centuries. Identify the following locations on Map 15-2 on page 311 of your textbook and place them on the map provided on the next page of this *Study Guide*.

1. Papal States

2. Italy

3. German States

4. France

5. Burgundy

6. Avignon

7. Rome

8. Aachen

9. Augsburg

10. Florence

11. Assisi

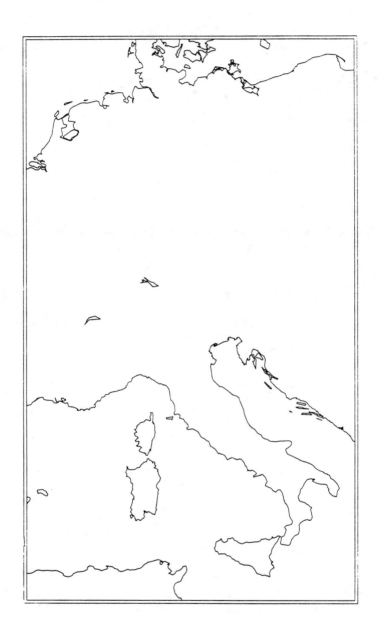

MULTIPLE CHOICE ANSWER KEY *(with page references)*

1. D (298)

2. B (299)

3. A (299)

4. C (300)

5. D (301)

6. B (304)

7. C (310)

8. B (306)

9. D (310)

10. C (310)

11. A (312)

12. A (312)

13. D (314)

14. B (314)

15. A (315)

16. C (299)

17. B (299)

18. A (301)

19. B (302)

20. C (304)

21. A (305)

22. D (306)

23. C (309)

24. B (319)

25. D (321)

Chapter Sixteen
The Age of Reformation and Religious Wars

Practice Test

1. For Europe, the late fifteenth and the sixteenth centuries were a period of
    a. unprecedented territorial expansion
    b. ideological experimentation
    c. social engineering and political planning
    d. all of the above

2. Columbus' voyage of 1492 marked the
    a. beginning of three centuries of Spanish conquest and exploitation
    b. beginning of a process that virtually destroyed the native civilizations of America
    c. rise of Spain to a major political role in Europe
    d. all of the above

3. The flood of spices and precious metals that flowed back into Europe over new trade routes
    a. contributed to a steady rise in prices during the sixteenth century
    b. contributed to a sudden rise in prices
    c. allowed prices to fall gradually as manufacturing was increased
    d. resulted in the institution of mercantilism

4. The most famous of the northern Humanists was
    a. Francisco Jimenez de Cisneros   c. Voltaire
    b. Desiderius Erasmus   d. Ulrich Zwingli

5. *Utopia* by Thomas More
    a. was a theological tract that supported the Catholic church
    b. depicted an imaginary society based on reason and tolerance
    c. was an exposé of human self-deception
    d. was a simple work that supported ethical piety in imitation of Christ

6. An indulgence was
    a. a payment to obtain an office in the church
    b. a punishment meted out by the pope to heretics
    c. forgiveness given by the pope exclusively to Protestants in order to entice them back to the church
    d. none of the above

7. Which of the following was a pamphlet written by Martin Luther?
    a. *Address to the Christian Nobility of the German Nation*
    b. *The Praise of Folly*
    c. *Institutes of the Christian Religion*
    d. *Spiritual Exercises*

8. The Diet of Worms declared that
    a. the pope's spiritual authority exceeded the temporal power of the emperor
    b. the writings of Erasmus were to be placed on the *Index of Forbidden Books*
    c. Martin Luther was to be placed under the imperial ban and considered an outlaw
    d. both a and b

9. The Peasant Revolt of 1524 was
    a. successful in freeing the peasantry from feudal obligations
    b. supported by Martin Luther as a "Christian enterprise"
    c. condemned by Martin Luther as "unchristian" and crushed by German princes
    d. important in demonstrating that Luther was a social revolutionary

10. The reformation in Zurich was led by
    a. John Calvin   c. Philip of Hesse
    b. Ulrich Zwingli   d. Menno Simons

11. The Peace of Augsburg recognized in law what had already been established in practice:
    a. the religion of the land was determined by the Holy Roman Emperor
    b. Calvinists were to be tolerated throughout Europe
    c. Protestants everywhere must readopt old Catholic beliefs and practices
    d. the ruler of a land would determine the religion of the land

12. Calvin and his followers
    a. were motivated by a desire to transform society morally
    b. promoted a belief that only the "elect" would be saved
    c. did not depend on strict laws for governing Geneva
    d. both a and b

13. The Council of Trent (1545-1563)
    a. weakened the authority of local bishops in religious matters
    b. took steps to curtail the selling of Church offices
    c. took no steps to improve the image of parish priests
    d. changed the basic tenets of the Catholic church

14. The "King's Affair" refers to
    a. the attempt by Henry VIII to divorce Catherine of Aragon and marry Anne Boleyn
    b. Henry VIII's establishment of the Anglican church
    c. the illegitimate children fathered by Henry VIII
    d. the execution of Sir Thomas More

15. Thomas Hobbes was an important political philosopher who
    a. wrote *Treatise on Religious and Political Philosophy*
    b. argued that freedom of thought was essential to true liberty
    c. believed that people should live in a tightly controlled commonwealth
    d. both a and b

16. In what ways did the Reformation change religious life?
    a. There were more clergy than before the Reformation
    b. The clergy could marry
    c. There were more churches and religious holidays than before the Reformation
    d. Local shrines became more popular

17. Protestants stressed, as no religious movement before them,
    a. individualism and egalitarianism
    b. the sacredness of home and family
    c. the sacredness of celibacy
    d. the inequality of men and women

18. After the Council of Trent adjourned in 1563
    a. Catholics were able to peacefully coexist with Protestants
    b. many Protestants returned to Catholicism
    c. Catholics began a Jesuit-led counteroffensive against Protestants
    d. both a and b

19. The term Huguenot refers to
    a. a French Protestant
    b. a French Catholic
    c. a powerful French family
    d. the French royal family

20. The Edict of Nantes
    a. outlawed Protestantism in France
    b. assured equal treatment of Protestants and Catholics in France
    c. made Calvinist Protestantism the official religion of France
    d. assured limited rights to Protestants in Catholic France

21. A *politique*
    a. places political autonomy and well-being above religious creeds
    b. places equal emphasis on political autonomy and religious creeds
    c. believes political autonomy requires religious uniformity
    d. believes that religion has no role in politics

22. The Thirty Years' War
    a. was the last and most destructive of the wars of religion
    b. involved virtually every major European land
    c. shaped much of the map of northern Europe as we know it today
    d. did not involve Protestant estates in Germany

23. The essential foundation of the great witch hunts of the sixteenth century was
    a. the popular belief in science
    b. the strong Christian culture of rural villages
    c. the popular belief in magic
    d. d. both a and b

24. Blaise Paschal
    a. was a French playwright
    b. was a French mathematician
    c. was a follower of Calvin
    d. was the most controversial thinker of the seventeenth century

25. The most influential thinker of the seventeenth century has proved to be
    a. John Locke
    b. Baruch Spinoza
    c. Thomas Hobbes
    d. Blaise Paschal

When

1. How long after the posting of the 95 theses did the Council of Trent convene?

110

2. How long after the posting of the 95 theses was Lutheranism recognized at the Peace of Augsburg?

3. Place the following terms in events into correct order: Act of Supremacy, Reformation Parliament, Act of Conformity, Submission of the Clergy, Act of Succession.

Where

Using Map 16-1 on page 331 of your textbook, match the explorers to the appropriate voyage.

1. Cartier_____   a. first European to sail to India

2. Magellan_____   b. east coast of North America

3. Cabot_____   c. Newfoundland

4. Columbus_____   d. completed circumnavigation of the globe

5. Elcano_____   e. discovered the New World

6. Da Gama_____   f. died circumnavigating the globe

How and Why

1.   What were the principal problems within the church that contributed to the Protestant Reformation? Why was the church unable to suppress dissent as it had earlier?

2.	Was the Reformation a fundamentally religious phenomenon or a generally broader development? To what extent were economic, social,and cultural factors involved in the origins and spread of the Reformation? How can emphasis of the religious or nonreligious character of the period alter the conception of the Reformation?

3.	What were the basic similarities and differences between the ideas of Luther and Zwingli? Luther and Calvin? Did the differences tend to split the Protestant ranks and thereby lessen the effectiveness of the movement?

4.	What was the Counter-Reformation and what principal decisions and changes were instituted by the Council of Trent? Was the Protestant Reformation a healthy movement for the Catholic church?

5. Why did Henry VIII finally break with the Catholic church? What "new" religion did he establish and what were its basic precepts? Did this solve the problem? What new problems did his successors face as a result of Henry's move? What was Elizabeth I's settlement and how difficult was it to impose upon all of England?

6. Why was the Thirty Years' War fought? To what extent did politics determine the outcome of the war? Discuss the Treaty of Westphalia in 1648. Could matters have been resolved without war?

Map Labeling

By 1600, religious allegiance was divided among four branches of Christianity. By using Map 16-2 on page 353 of your textbook and the map provided on the next page , identify the areas dominated by the Roman Catholic Church or by one of the three largest Protestant churches, noting which church it was.

1. Lutheran   3. Anglican

2. Calvinist   4. Roman Catholic

113

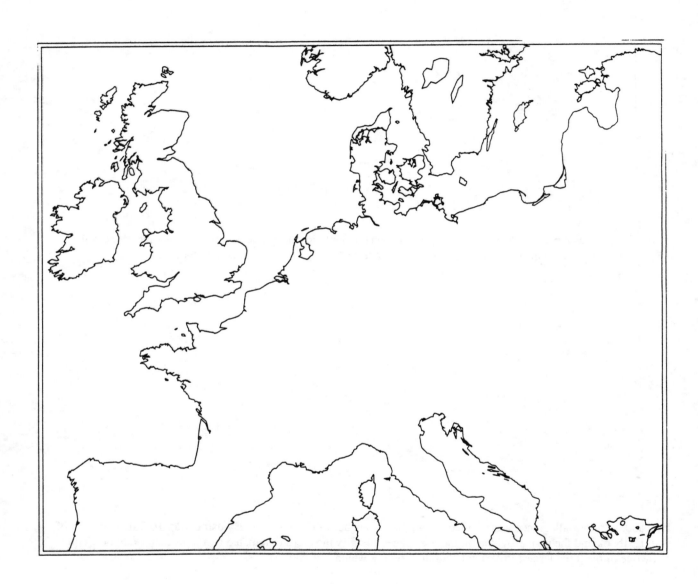

MULTIPLE CHOICE ANSWER KEY *(with page references)*

1. D (330)

2. C (332)

3. A (332)

4. B (334)

5. B (334)

6. D (335)

7. A (337)

8. C (337)

9. C (338)

10. B (338)

11. D (341)

12. D (346)

13. B (344)

14. A (341)

15. C (362)

16. B (345)

17. B (346)

18. C (348)

19. A (349)

20. D (351)

21. A (349)

22. D (354)

23. C (358)

24. B (361)

25. A (364)

Chapter Seventeen
Africa (ca. 1000-1800)

Practice Test

1. By 1800, Islamic influence in sub-Saharan Africa
   - a. extended as far south as Zimbabwe
   - c. had penetrated through all levels of society
   - b. eliminated indigenous idea
   - d. both b and c

2. After the sixteenth century, which political power controlled most of North Africa?
   - a. Mamluk Empire
   - c. Ottoman Empire
   - b. Sharifian Empire
   - d. Tunisian Empire

3. Muslim conversion in West and Central Africa was primarily due to the
   - a. influence of Muslim traders
   - b. breakdown of state-sponsored religion
   - c. absence of hostile Berbers from the region
   - d. Arabian fanatics

4. Which of the following West African rulers converted to Islam in the 1030s?
   - a. Fulbe
   - c. Kilwa
   - b. Mossi
   - d. Tripoli

5. After the conquest of North Africa by the Ottomans
   - a. regionalism was crushed
   - c. regionalism persisted
   - b. Morocco lost its independence
   - d. Egyptian power never recovered

6. Which of the following developed into a notable and long-lived kingdom in the West and Central Sudan?
   - a. Ghana
   - c. Songhai
   - b. Mali
   - d. all of the above

7. In the late twelfth century, the Ghanaian state was destroyed
   - a. by Berber raiders
   - b. because of the failure of overland trade routes
   - c. by fanatical Almoravids
   - d. by anti-Muslim Soso people

8. The greatest Keita king proved to be
   - a. Sundiata
   - c. Mansa Musa
   - b. Gao
   - d. Askia Muhammad al-Turi

9. The major source of wealth for the Songhai kingdom was the
   - a. coastal trade with the south
   - b. ivory trade with the east
   - c. caravan trade across the Sahara to the north
   - d. both a and c

10. The architect of the Kanem empire in central Sudan was
    - a. Sokoto
    - c. Maqurra
    - b. Mai Dunama Dibbalemi
    - d. Alwa

11. A significant factor in the gradual disappearance of Christianity in the Nubian region was
    a. the apparently elite character of Christianity there
    b. the eradication of its churches by hostile tribal leaders
    c. its association with the foreign Egyptian world of Coptic Christianity
    d. both a and c

12. The lasting significance of Benin lies in its
    a. court art
    b. government hierarchy
    c. political history
    d. focus on human sacrifice

13. *Trekboers* were
    a. nomadic white livestock farmers in South Africa
    b. slave traders in South Africa
    c. British governmental representatives
    d. representatives of the Dutch East India Company

14. King Alfonso I of Kongo
    a. suppressed all Christianity in his kingdom
    b. halted the slave trade in his kingdom
    c. consolidated his government and remained a Christian
    d. both and c

15. The Portuguese arrival in southeastern Africa during the first years of the sixteenth century
    a. led to the establishment of the Great Zimbabwe civilization
    b. was important for establishing Swahili control of the inland gold trade
    c. led to the establishment of the *apartheid* system that was so destructive to the region
    d. was catastrophic for the East African coastal economy

16. The mainstays of the Mali economy were
    a. agriculture and war
    b. agriculture and trade
    c. trade and war
    d. agriculture and alliances with the Portuguese

17. Arguably, the most powerful African state in the late fifteenth and early sixteenth centuries was
    a. Ghana
    b. Benin
    c. Songhai
    d. Mali

18. Idris Alawa was able to unify Kanem and Bornu through
    a. the support of Islamic culture
    b. the use of firearms
    c. the help of Turkish military instructors
    d. both b and c

19. The gradual involvement of Africa in the emerging global economic system
    a. brought unprecedented wealth to the continent
    b. paved the way for colonial domination
    c. led to a resurgence of Christianity throughout the continent
    d. both a and c

20. Trade between the Portuguese and Kongo
    a. augmented the prestige of the Kongo elite
    b. eventually centered on the slave trade
    c. led to the Christianization of Kongo
    d. both a and b

21. Swahili
    a. developed from the interaction of Bantu and Arabic speakers
    b. was replaced by Arabic as Islam spread throughout East Africa
    c. developed from the interaction of Bantu and Portuguese speakers
    d. is the Spanish and Portuguese term for Muslims

22. The decline of Swahili civilization in the sixteenth century can be attributed primarily to
    a. the arrival of the Dutch East India Company
    b. Arab dominance of the Indian Ocean trade
    c. the arrival of the Portuguese
    d. Bantu migrations

23. "Great Zimbabwe" refers to
    a. an impressive set of ruins in southeastern Africa
    b. the Portuguese name for southeastern Africa
    c. the Dutch name for southeastern Africa
    d. both a and c

24. The Omanis
    a. were a Swahili tribe who ousted the Portuguese from East Africa north of Mozambique
    b. were the eastern Arabians that ousted the Portuguese from East Africa north of Mozambique
    c. fueled a recovery of prosperity in East Africa
    d. both b and c

25. The Dutch East India Company established the Cape Colony
    a. to extract slaves from the interior for sale in the Americas
    b. as a refueling station between the Netherlands and the East Indies
    c. to more effectively support the Trekboers in their conflict with the Khoikhoi
    d. to contest Portuguese power in East Africa

When

1. Place the following Sahelian empires in chronological order: Mali, Songhai, Ghana.

2. When was the Kongo kingdom founded? How long after that was the arrival of the Portuguese?

3. According to the chronologies in this chapter, which African state survived the longest? How long did it survive?

118

Where

Study Map 17-1 on page 370 of your textbook and compare it with Map 17-2 on page 374. What changes have taken place from 900 to 1800 in Africa regarding trade routes and the political control of different empires? Note in particular the inset maps of the region of West Africa.

How and Why

1. What was the importance of the Ghana, Mali, and Songhai empires to world history? Why was the control of trade across the Sahara so important to these kingdoms? What was the importance of Muslim culture to these groups? Why did all of the empires fail in these regions?

2. What was the impact of the Portuguese on the east coast of Africa? Why was this European power able to gain control of certain coastal areas in this region? What was the impact on the interior of Africa because of this development?

3. Describe the political situation of northern Africa in the eighteenth century. Why did Ottoman influence decline in this region?

4.   What was the "Great Zimbabwe" civilization and where did it take place? What are some of the reasons for the flowering of this civilization? What were the reasons for its demise?

5.   Discuss the diversity of Cape society in South Africa. Who were the Trekboers and what was their conflict with the Khoikhoi? How was the basis for apartheid formed at this time?

Map Labeling

Identify the following regions, peoples, and states of Africa from about 1500-1800 on Map 17-2 on page 374 of your textbook and place them on the map provided on the next page.

1. Ghanaian Empire	7. Luba
2. Asante	8. Lunda
3. Akan	9. Ndongo
4. Songhai	10. Shona
5. Hausa States	11. Changamire
6. Kongo	12. Cape Colony

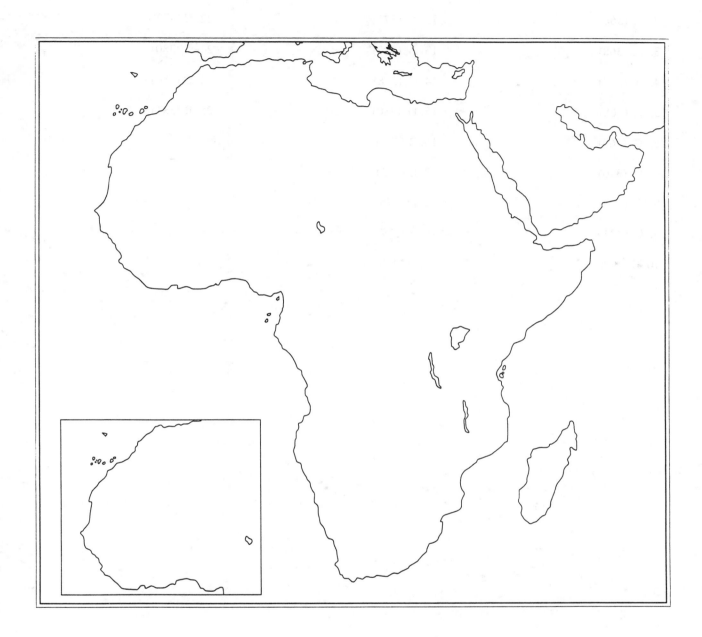

MULTIPLE CHOICE ANSWER KEY *(with page references)*

1. A (368)
2. C (368)
3. A (368)
4. A (368)
5. C (368)
6. D (369)
7. D (370)
8. C (373)
9. C (374)
10. B (375)

11. D (376)
12. A (376)
13. A (382)
14. C (378)
15. D (380)
16. B (371)
17. C (373)
18. D (375)
19. B (377)
20. D (378)

21. A (379)
22. C (379)
23. A (380)
24. D (380)
25. B (381)

Chapter Eighteen
Conquest and Exploitation:
The Development of the Transatlantic Economy

Practice Test

1. Mercantilism
   a. encouraged free markets to increase national wealth
   b. regulated trade to increase national wealth
   c. regarded the world as an arena of unlimited wealth
   d. both a and c

2. In the New World, *audiencias* were
   a. judicial councils
   b. governors
   c. jails for smugglers
   d. religious audiences

3. In the New World, *conquistadores* were
   a. foot soldiers
   b. municipal councils
   c. local officers
   d. judicial councils

4. *Creoles* were
   a. people of mixed racial composition
   b. those born in the New World whose ancestry was European
   c. slaves from Central America who were sold in Caribbean ports
   d. those whose status improved due to reforms by Charles III

5. The African slave trade
   a. was rather narrow in its scope, directed as it was toward European markets
   b. must be seen as a part of a larger commercial system
   c. was directed to the exploitation of the New World
   d. both b and c

6. All the English colonies in North America were Protestant except
   a. Massachusetts
   b. Maryland
   c. Virginia
   d. Georgia

7. The *encomienda* was a
   a. land grant
   b. formal grant by the crown to the labor of a specific number of Native Americans for a particular time
   c. complicated system of bullion trade
   d. trading contract

8. The Spanish crown
   a. advocated the *encomienda* system
   b. voluntarily destroyed the *encomienda* system in the seventeenth century
   c. disliked the *encomienda* system because it created a powerful independent nobility in the New World
   d. both b and c

9. The Spanish monarchy received approval from Catholic church authorities for a policy of military conquest in Latin America
    a. only with strict guidelines against exploiting the native population
    b. upon signing the Treaty of Tordesillas
    c. on the grounds that conversion to Christianity justified actions of the state
    d. both a and b

10. Religious conversion of Native Americans by the Catholic church
    a. brought acceptance of European culture
    b. resulted in a very large percentage of Native Americans in the priesthood
    c. represented an attempt to destroy another part of Native American culture
    d. both a and b

11. By far the most effective and outspoken clerical critic of the Spanish conquistadors was
    a. Bartolomé de Las Casas   c. Jimenez de Cisneros
    b. Junipero Serra   d. none of the above

12. One of the most important forces that led to the spread of slavery in Brazil and the West Indies was the
    a. cultivation of tobacco   c. *encomienda* system
    b. cultivation of sugar   d. presence of small landowners in these areas

13. African slaves who were transported to the Americas
    a. generally converted to various Christian religious sects
    b. converted only to Protestantism
    c. maintained their African religions
    d. rejected their old religions and accepted the nature gods of the New World

14. The institution of slavery persisted in the Americas until the
    a. eighteenth century   c. nineteenth century
    b. twentieth century   d. seventeenth century

15. In Brazil, the economy was
    a. more dependent on Indian labor than in Spanish America
    b. less dependent on Indian labor than in Spanish America
    c. stable without slavery
    d. strictly regulated by the government

16. The European empires of the sixteenth through the eighteenth centuries existed primarily to
    a. enrich trade
    b. spread Christianity
    c. bring prestige to the European ruling class
    d. both a and c

17. The Roman Catholic Church in the New World
    a. was a major obstacle to Spanish and Portuguese economic interests
    b. was a conservative force protecting the interests of the Spanish authorities
    c. did not attempt to convert Native Americans
    d. sought to preserve Native American culture

18. Small military forces were able to defeat two advanced Native American cultures because of
    a. advanced weapons
    b. the susceptibility of natives to diseases like smallpox
    c. superior culture
    d. both a and b

19. In 1494, by the Treaty of Tordesillas, the pope
    a. granted Brazil to Portugal
    b. restricted slavery in the New World
    c. divided the empires of Spain and Portugal
    d. both a and c

20. The Portuguese empire in the New World differed from the Spanish in that
    a. Portugal depended more heavily on Native American labor
    b. Portugal had fewer resources to devote to its empire
    c. Portugal did not allow private persons to exploit the region
    d. Portugal did not use slaves

21. The relationship between English colonists and Native Americans can best be described as
    a. complex
    b. guided by missionary zeal
    c. disdainful
    d. violent

22. By the late seventeenth century, slavery
    a. had declined in Spanish South America
    b. increased in Spanish South America
    c. continued to prosper in Brazil and the West Indies
    d. both a and c

23. In the trans-Atlantic system, the Americas supplied
    a. manufactured goods
    b. slaves
    c. labor-intensive raw materials
    d. precious metals

24. The trade that supplied African slaves to Islamic lands is called the
    a. occidental slave trade
    b. the oriental slave trade
    c. the Arab slave trade
    d. both b and c

25. The principal carriers of the slave trade were the
    a. Spanish
    b. English
    c. Portuguese
    d. French

Where

Analyze Map 18-1 on page 391 of your textbook. What is a viceroyalty and how did Spain effectively rule its land claims in the Americas? Do you think Spain was overextended? What competitors did it face? Explain why such organization was necessary according to mercantilist theories.

How and Why

1.   How did the Spanish organize their empire in the Americas? Was this an efficient operation economically?

2.   What role did the Catholic Church play in the pacification of Native American civilizations?

3.   Describe the *encomienda* system. How did it differ from the *repartimiento*? Why was the *hacienda* such a dominant institution in rural and agricultural life?

4.   Describe the Atlantic slave trade. Where were slaves obtained and how were they treated? How did slavery affect the economy of the transatlantic trade?

5.   Discuss mercantilism in theory and practice. What were its main ideas? Did they work? Which European country was most successful in establishing a mercantilist empire? Why?

6.   How did the triangles of trade function among the Americas, Europe, and Africa?

Map Labeling

Study Map 18-1 on page 391 of your textbook and review page 389-393. On the map provided, shade in the areas controlled by Spain and draw the boundaries of Spanish viceroyalties. Label the areas in the New World controlled by European powers other than Spain or contested by European powers other than Spain.

MULTIPLE CHOICE ANSWER KEY *(with page references)*

1. B (386)

2. A (390)

3. A (389)

4. B (390)

5. D (395)

6. B (393)

7. B (390)

8. C (390)

9. C (388)

10. C (388)

11. A (388)

12. B (393)

13. A (395)

14. C (397)

15. B (393)

16. A (386)

17. B (387)

18. D (387)

19. C (292)

20. B (392)

21. A (393)

22. D (394)

23. C (394)

24. B (396)

25. C (396)

LECTURE COMPANION

The following lecture note pages can be used to record your instructor's lectures and assignments for each chapter.

Chapter 1
THE BIRTH OF CIVILIZATION

Lecture Notes   **Date:**_____

Chapter 2
THE FOUR GREAT REVOLUTIONS IN THOUGHT AND RELIGION

Lecture Notes   **Date:**_____

Chapter 3
GREEK AND HELLENISTIC CIVILIZATION

Lecture Notes   **Date:**_____

Chapter 4
IRAN, INDIA, AND INNER ASIA TO 200 C.E.

Lecture Notes   Date:_____

Chapter 5
REPUBLICAN AND IMPERIAL ROME

Lecture Notes   **Date:**_____

Chapter 6
AFRICA: EARLY HISTORY TO 1000 C.E.

Lecture Notes   Date:_____

Chapter 7
CHINA'S FIRST EMPIRE (221 B.C.E.- 220 C.E.)

Lecture Notes

Date:_____

Chapter 8
IMPERIAL CHINA (589-1368)

Lecture Notes   Date:_____

Chapter 9
JAPAN: EARLY HISTORY TO 1467

Lecture Notes   Date:_____

Chapter 10
IRAN AND INDIA BEFORE ISLAM

Lecture Notes   Date:_____

Chapter 11
THE FORMATION OF ISLAMIC CIVILIZATION (622-945)

Lecture Notes

Date:_____

Chapter 12
THE EARLY MIDDLE AGES IN THE WEST TO 1000: THE BIRTH OF EUROPE

Lecture Notes   Date:_____

Chapter 13
THE ISLAMIC HEARTLANDS AND INDIA (ca. 1000-1500)

Lecture Notes   **Date:**_____

Lecture Notes   Date:_____

Chapter 15
EUROPE TO THE EARLY 1500s: REVIVAL, DECLINE, AND RENAISSANCE

Lecture Notes   **Date:**_____

Chapter 16
THE AGE OF REFORMATION AND RELIGIOUS WARS

Lecture Notes

Date:_____

Chapter 17
AFRICA (ca. 1000-1800)

Lecture Notes

Date:_____

Chapter 18
CONQUEST AND EXPLOITATION:
THE DEVELOPMENT OF THE TRANSATLANTIC ECONOMY

Lecture Notes   **Date:**_____